GW00338402

Cuba

Front cover and right: Vintage
American cars are a regular
sight on the streets of Cuba

TOP 10 ATTRACTIONS

Music • In various traditional styles, live music can be heard all over the island (page 83)

Beaches • Beautiful white-sand beaches abound, from Varadero to Playa Esmeralda, Playa Ancón to Cayo Levisa

Baracoa • A pleasant coastal town in the far east of Cuba (page 80)

Cathedral Square • An impressive stage set at the heart of the Old City of Havana (page 27)

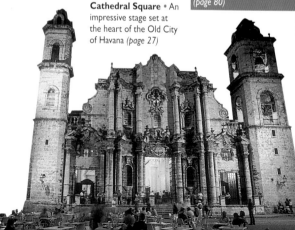

Casa Museo de Ernest Hemingway – Where things remain just as the author left them (page 44)

El Morro – Santiago's well-preserved fort (page 77)

Trinidad – Frozen in time, this city is an enchanting colonial gem and a World Heritage Site (page 59)

Viñales Valley – Visit tobacco fields and *mogotes* (page 48)

Camagüey – The streets and squares of Cuba's third city have been restored to their former glory (page 66)

The Prado – Grand old buildings flank the loveliest avenue in Old Havana (page 37)

CONTENTS

87

93

10

32

39

70

Features

INTRODUCTION

The largest island in the Caribbean, Cuba is blessed with palm trees, sultry temperatures, hip-swivelling rhythms, pristine beaches, a surfeit of rum and the world's finest hand-rolled cigars. But it's nearly impossible to think of Cuba only in those hedonistic terms – even if you're merely headed to one of the island's tourist resorts.

For much of the 20th century, Cuba occupied a leading role on the world stage wholly disproportionate to its small size and lack of economic clout. From the overthrow of the dictator Fulgencio Batista at the end of 1958 to Fidel Castro's tenacious hold on power and declarations of socialism, this small Caribbean nation has assumed near-mythical status as a living laboratory of social experimentation, political defiance and a people's perseverance.

Legacy of the Revolution

For nearly half a century a combative Fidel Castro weathered the opposition of the US government and the hostility of Cuban exiles in Miami. The new president, his brother Raúl, continues his legacy with a few modifications. The Cuban people were required to make repeated sacrifices in the face of the ongoing American trade embargo and the collapse of the Soviet Union's support and trade. Cuba is still standing, and despite the hardships has even managed to restore many of its fine colonial buildings.

As one of the last Communist hold-outs in the world, this nation is an enduring curiosity. With much of the rest of the planet racing ahead at a dizzying digital pace, Cuba crawls along in a slow-motion time warp. Behemoth vintage American cars from the 1940s and 1950s, patched and propped up, lumber down the streets of dimly lit cities. In rural areas cars give way to oxen-led carts, wobbly iron bicycles and pedicabs. Houses are equipped with the most rudimentary, ancient appliances imaginable. And musicians play wonderfully addictive Cuban *son*, rhythms unchanged since the 1930s.

Cuba is inseparable from the politics of the latter half of the 20th century. Children are sworn in at the age of six to become Young Communist Pioneers. Throughout the country giant billboards function like pep talks from the government, proclaiming '*Socialismo o Muerte*' ('Socialism or Death') and '*Viva la Revolución*' ('Long Live the Revolution'). Portraits of Che Guevara, the 1960s revolutionary martyr, are plastered on the walls of shops, offices and homes.

Cuban Reality

Everything has always creaked and sputtered in hard-pressed Communist Cuba. However, the last few years have seen the economy revive, and things are now better than in the immediate post-Soviet years. But many families continue to live in overcrowded conditions, and most people earn less than the equivalent of US$25 a month.

The Face of Cuba

Cuba's 11 million people have a distinctively mixed heritage that reflects the twists and turns of the island's history. The first black slaves were brought over in the early 16th century to replace an indigenous population that was being wiped out (see page 12). But immigration from Spain did not start in earnest until the late 18th century, when the sugar industry boomed. Plantation owners – both local Spanish as well as French immigrants from Haiti – brought thousands of slaves from West Africa, who were supplemented by Chinese labourers after slavery was abolished in 1886. During the last 200 years the various ethnic groups have interbred and today about 51 percent of Cubans are *mulatos* (mixed race).

In the early 1990s Castro needed to reorganise the economy after the collapse of the Eastern Bloc which had formerly subsidised Cuba. In 1993 it became legal for Cubans to hold US currency. Much of the economy was given over to the almighty dollar, with many products and foodstuffs available only in dollar stores. Cubans with family members abroad who could send remittances, or with jobs in foreign businesses or tourism which pro-

Eating ice-cream in Havana

vided tips or wages in US currency, soon had the advantage over those with no access to dollars. A decade later there was a deepening split between the haves and have-nots and Castro was forced to take action to halt the division. All foreign currency now has to be exchanged for *pesos convertibles* and there is a steep tax on converting US dollars. Poverty has been tackled by doubling the minimum wage and trebling pensions.

The glaring deficiencies of the Cuban economy and needs of the Cuban people are impossible to ignore. Cubans also enjoy no real freedom of speech, freedom of the press or freedom to travel outside the country, although Raúl is relaxing some restrictions. Still, one doesn't see the blinding, heart-wrenching poverty in Cuba common in places like Bangladesh, India and even other parts of Latin America. Housing is provided by the state – you are unlikely to see homeless people sleeping on the streets anywhere in Cuba – and while Cubans don't get nearly enough with their ration books, they have something to eat. All Cubans are entitled to free health care, and education is free

Trinidad landscape

and available to all. Average life expectancy rose from 57 years in 1958 to over 77 years in 2007 – the 14th highest in the world.

Cuba's dilapidation, poverty and restrictions only serve to highlight the indomitable spirit of the Cuban people. They are blessed with a remarkable resiliency, forbearance and joy that no economic hardship seems capable of diminishing. Cubans are as hospitable a people as you'll find, inviting visitors into their cramped homes given half a chance. Everywhere there are bubbly school children – outfitted in identical maroon or mustard-coloured uniforms – racing around the streets, playing pick-up games of stickball, or amusing themselves with improvised skateboards and kites.

Paradise Island

In dire need of hard currency, Cuba embraced tourism, which has now surpassed the sugar industry to become the country's top revenue earner. It's obvious why, for many Cuba is first and foremost an idyllic sun-and-sea bolt-hole. The white sandy beaches are dazzling, with the long shores of Varadero in the north perhaps the best known. Other stars of Cuban beach tourism include Guardalavaca, its neighbour, Playa Esmeralda, and the islands of Cayo Largo and Cayo Coco. Amateur sailors appreciate the countless natural harbours, anglers search for marlin off the coast, while scuba divers explore the many coral reefs and sunken wrecks.

Most travellers still opt for package tours, but Cuba's great diversity of attractions is tempting an increasing number away from the sea and sand. In the island's eastern corner is Cuba's highest mountain range, the Sierra Maestra (up to 1,974m/ 6,476ft), site of many uprisings and rebellions; to the west, in Pinar del Río province, is the verdant Viñales Valley with its huge *mogotes*, limestone rocks up to 400m (1,300ft) high; and central Cuba has the lush Sierra del Escambray mountains and the old sugar-cane plantations of the Valle de los Ingenios.

Then there are the towns and cities. There's Havana, of course – a place with a magical appeal, combining fine Spanish colonial architecture, vibrant street life and a range of cultural opportunities; Trinidad, a gorgeous colonial-era gem, its town houses, churches and other fine buildings set on winding, cobblestone streets; and Santiago de Cuba, a lively and colourful Cuban cocktail of Spanish, French and African cultures.

Playa Ancón near Trinidad

A BRIEF HISTORY

When Christopher Columbus disembarked on eastern Cuba on 27 October 1492, he penned a note exclaiming that the land was 'the most lovely that eyes have ever seen'. Indigenous groups including the Ciboney from Central and South America had lived on the island since at least 3500BC.

In 1511 Diego Velázquez sailed from neighbouring Hispaniola with some 300 conquistadors. Baracoa became the first of seven settlements across Cuba. Velázquez and his followers enslaved the native peoples and in the process exposed them to European diseases. Entire villages committed suicide, and by the mid-1500s the native population had declined from over 150,000 to just 3,000.

Morro fort, Havana

Piracy and Trade

Until the end of the 16th century, Cuba remained a fairly insignificant Spanish colony. The port cities of Havana and Santiago de Cuba were heavily fortified to defend against French and English pirate raids.

From the 17th century Havana became increasingly significant as a stopover point for treasure fleets. In 1762 British forces captured the city. They held it for only a year before returning it to Spain in exchange for Florida, but during this period trade was opened up to additional markets, notably the North American colonies. A lucrative tobacco industry had taken hold in Cuba, and after 1763 the sugar industry skyrocketed. Though settlers brought the first African slaves to Cuba

Sugar island

By the middle of the 19th century, Cuba produced a third of the world's sugar and was considered one of the most valuable colonies in the world. Half a million slaves – nearly half the population – worked the plantations, and at least 3,500 trading ships visited Cuba annually.

in the early 1500s, hundreds of thousands of African slaves were imported in the late 18th and 19th centuries to meet the demands of the plantation industry.

The Road to Independence

Spaniards born and raised in Cuba, known as *criollos* (creoles), managed the sugar-cane plantations but were not involved in the running of the country. During the 19th century some criollos (particularly in Oriente, the island's poorer, eastern region) became increasingly disenchanted and desired greater autonomy. On 10 October 1868 Carlos Manuel de Céspedes, a criollo plantation owner, issued a call for independence and liberated the slaves from his estate, La Demajagua. During the subsequent Ten Years' War (1868–78) 50,000 Cubans – including Céspedes – and more than 200,000 Spanish lost their lives. Cuba remained a colony of Spain, but the war contributed to the abolition of slavery on the island in 1886 and cemented national consciousness.

In 1895 José Martí, Cuba's most venerated patriot (who now has a street, square or building named after him in every town), led the next and most important uprising against Spain. Born in 1853 and exiled at 18 for his political views,

José Martí Memorial in Havana

Martí became a journalist and poet. From exile in the United States he argued for Cuban independence. Martí was killed in an ambush during the War of Independence, which began in 1895 and in which some 300,000 Cubans lost their lives.

Throughout the 19th century, the United States, which was keenly interested in the island's strategic significance and its sugar market, had become increasingly involved in Cuban affairs. A US purchase of the island from Spain had long been on the agenda, even though Martí had warned of the dangers of becoming a satellite of the United States ('I know the Monster, because I have lived in its lair,' he wrote).

In February 1898 the USS *Maine* was sunk in Havana's harbour, killing all 260 crew members. Although it was most likely caused by an accidental explosion in the hold, the United States used the sinking as a pretext to declare war. US victory in the Spanish-American War came swiftly, with Spain surrendering its claim to the island by the end of the same year. A US provisional military government lasted until 1902, when Cuba became an independent republic. But the country was still subject to US military intervention – as a result of the Platt Amendment to the Cuban constitution – which many claim hamstrung true independence.

False Independence

For the next five decades the United States, the largest importer of Cuban sugar, dominated the island's economy and largely controlled its political processes. The period was rife with political corruption, violence and terrorism. After 1933 Fulgencio Batista, though only a sergeant, controlled the strings of power through a series of puppet presidents before winning the presidency outright in 1940. He retired in 1944 but returned by staging a military coup in 1952. His dictatorship made it possible for him to invest some $300 million abroad by 1959.

Since the 1920s disillusionment with the nascent republic – with its clear dependence on the United States and its lack of political probity or social equality – had grown steadily. Although Cuba had the second-highest per capita income in Latin America, prosperity did not filter down from the upper classes. In fact, the World Bank in 1950 declared as many as 60 percent of Cubans undernourished. In Havana there was a greater concentration of millionaires than anywhere else in Central or South America, and the capital was dubbed 'an offshore Las Vegas' for its brothels, casinos and gangsters.

The Road to Revolution

On 26 July 1953, rebels attacked the Moncada Barracks in Santiago de Cuba. The assault failed, but it thrust into the limelight its young leader, Fidel Castro. Castro was imprisoned and put on trial in a closed hearing; his legendary two-hour defence speech, later published as *History Will Absolve Me*, became a revolutionary manifesto. Castro was incarcerated on the Isle of Pines (now called the Isla de la Juventud) until May 1955, when Batista granted an amnesty to political prisoners.

Castro then fled to Mexico. The following year he returned to southeastern Cuba with a force of 81 guerrillas (including Che Guevara) crammed onto a small yacht, the *Granma*. Only 15 reached the Sierra Maestra mountains safely. Incredibly, from such inauspicious beginnings the so-called '26 of July Movement' grew into a serious guerrilla army, aided in no small part by local peasants who were promised land reform.

Following a disastrous offensive by government troops on the rebels' mountain strongholds in 1958, and the capture of Santa Clara by Che Guevara and his men on 30 December,

Che and Fidel: Brothers in Revolution

Ernesto 'Che' Guevara (che meaning 'mate' or 'buddy' in Argentine slang) is the official poster boy and martyr of the Cuban Revolution, idolised by Cubans. His dramatic, beret-topped visage is seen on billboards and photographs throughout Cuba. Born in 1928 in Argentina, Guevara trained as a doctor before embarking on nomadic treks through South and Central America with a pile of Marxist literature in his rucksack. He met Castro in Mexico in 1955 and for the next 10 years was Castro's right-hand man, as a guerrilla in the mountains then as director of the national bank (signing bills as, simply, 'Che'), minister of industry, and minister of the economy. In 1965, he abandoned Cuba for new causes. He was killed trying to foment revolt in Bolivia in 1967.

Fidel Castro – for 49 years the president of Cuba, secretary-general of its Communist Party, and commander-in-chief of its armed forces – was born in 1926 and trained as a lawyer at the University of Havana. The world's youngest leader in 1959, Castro defied all expectations to become one of the longest-serving heads of state on the planet. Fidel, as he is known to all, was a towering but frustrating patriarchal figure to Cubans. Yet he remained, above all, El Comandante.

Fidel finally quit smoking cigars in 1985, saying they were great for the Cuban economy 'but not so great for my health'. In 2006, aged 80, he had to temporarily hand over power to his brother Raúl while undergoing abdominal surgery. His recovery was slow and the temporary arrangement became permanent in 2008. Fidel outlasted nine American presidents, despite a fabled list of CIA assassination attempts.

on 1 January 1959 Batista fled the country. The *barbudos* (the bearded ones) triumphantly entered Santiago, then marched into Havana one week later.

Fidel's Cuba

Castro's fledgling government immediately ordered rents reduced, new wage levels set, and estates limited in size to 390 hectares (966 acres). A nationalisation programme followed, and the government expropriated factories, utili-

Castro by Guayasamin

ties and more land. The foundations were set for near-universal state employment. At the same time, the government instituted programmes to eradicate illiteracy and provide free universal schooling and health care.

A centralised, all-powerful state didn't please all Cubans. The media were soon placed under state control, promised elections were never held, and Committees for the Defence of the Revolution (CDRs) were established to keep tabs on dissenters. In the early years of the Revolution, tens of thousands of people suspected of being unsympathetic to its goals were detained, imprisoned or sent to labor camps, along with such other 'undesirables' as homosexuals and priests.

Between 1959 and 1962 about 200,000 Cubans, primarily professionals and affluent landowners, fled the country. Expatriate Cubans settled in nearby Florida, establishing a colony that would steadily gain in political and economic power. Another 200,000 abandoned Cuba as part of the Freedom Flights Program between 1965 and 1971, some 125,000

Tank display at the Bay of Pigs

followed in 1980, when Castro lifted travel restrictions from the port of Mariel.

According to Washington estimates, US businesses lost $8 billion as a result of Cuba's state appropriations and seizing of assets. In 1961 CIA-trained Cuban exiles attempted an overthrow of Castro's regime, resulting in the Bay of Pigs fiasco.

The US remained fundamentally opposed to Cuba's political evolution and sought to isolate Castro in Latin America. Soon after the Bay of Pigs, Castro declared himself a Marxist-Leninist. Castro had not displayed any Communist inclinations in the 1950s, and some suggest that US aggression pushed him to ingratiate himself with the powerful Soviet Union and its Eastern bloc of potential trading partners. By the end of the 1980s, more than 80 percent of Cuban trade was with the USSR, which also provided Cuba with a subsidy of state support worth an estimated US$5 billion annually.

In 1962 Soviet president Nikita Khrushchev installed 42 medium-range nuclear missiles in Cuba. US president John F. Kennedy imposed a naval blockade on the island to ensure no more missiles arrived and insisted that the existing ones be removed. After six days of eyeball-to-eyeball challenge (now known in the US as the 'Cuban Missile Crisis'), Khrushchev backed down in return for the withdrawal of US nuclear missiles from Turkey. The same year saw the imposition of a total trade embargo by the US (which Cubans call the *bloqueo*), and which remains in force to this day.

The Special Period

Until the end of the 1980s, Soviet trade and subsidies were cru-
cial factors in propping up Cuba's heavily centralised and often
badly planned economy. But the subsequent dismantling of the
Soviet Union left Cuba bereft of food, oil and hard currency.
The government announced the start of a 'Special Period' in
1990, introducing new austerity measures. Though rationing
had existed since 1962, it was increased to cover many more
basic items. It became virtually impossible for Cubans to live
on rations alone. To make matters worse, in 1992 the Cuba
Democracy Act extended the US embargo to cover a ban on
trade with Cuba for foreign subsidiaries of US companies.

With its economy in disarray, the government introduced a
limited number of capitalist measures while maintaining a firm
political grip. Foreign investment, in the form of joint ventures
in the fields of tourism and mineral and oil exploration, was
keenly encouraged. The dollar was legalised in 1993.

Further measures, such as the legalisation of small enterprises
in 1993 and the introduction of farmers' markets in 1994,
improved the welfare of some Cubans. Life was still hard, however, and in August 1994 30,000 Cubans fled to Florida on

The Bay of Pigs Invasion

On 17 April 1961, a force of 1,297 Cuban exiles landed at Playa Girón. The
Cubans were CIA-trained and came from US ships waiting offshore; US-
piloted planes had bombed Cuban airfields days before. President Kennedy
was unwilling to commit US troops on the ground or order further air
strikes (US participation was denied at every stage). Castro's 20,000 troops,
assisted by artillery and tanks, repelled the invasion within 65 hours. Some
1,180 exiles were captured and ransomed for US$53 million worth of food
and medicine. The victory greatly boosted Castro's domestic and international status. Soon after, he declared Cuba a socialist, one-party state.

The ubiquitous image of Che

makeshift rafts. Today, the harshest days of privation have receded, although thousands still risk the open seas and a legal migration quota of 20,000 people a year is accepted into the US.

A New Era

Cuba now has new allies, chief of whom is the President of Venezuela, Hugo Chávez. Thousands of Cuban doctors have been sent to the *barrios* of Venezuela in return for cheap oil. Cuba remains a thorn in the side of the US administration due its close relations with countries such as Iran and China.

Castro turned 80 in 2006, but the event was overshadowed by the announcement that he was to hand power temporarily to his brother, Raúl, while he underwent surgery. After making a slow recovery, he was not strong enough to take up the reins of government again. In 2008 he declined to stand for re-election as president. Raúl was chosen as president of the Council of State and the Council of Ministers. His first measures were to lift a range of restrictions on consumer spending for those with access to foreign currency. Cubans may now own mobile phones and DVD players, rent cars and stay in tourist hotels on the beach. Some criminals had their death sentences commuted and two UN human rights treaties were signed after long being opposed by Fidel. Agriculture was decentralised and farmers given greater autonomy as part of a drive for greater production and efficiency. Raúl reorganised the leadership and consolidated his power as he pushed through the reforms.

Historical Landmarks

1492 Christopher Columbus lands in eastern Cuba.

1511 Diego Velázquez begins Spanish settlement.

1519 Havana, founded in 1515, moved to its present site.

1868–78 Ten Years' War for Cuban independence, ends with victory for Spanish forces.

1886 End of slavery in Cuba.

1895 War of Independence begins; José Martí killed.

1898 Sinking of the USS *Maine*; US defeats Spain, which surrenders Cuba to the US.

1902 Formation of the Republic of Cuba.

1940–44 Fulgencio Batista's first term as president.

1952 Batista seizes power again.

1953 Fidel Castro launches failed attack on the Moncada Barracks (26 July).

1959 Batista flees; Castro seizes power (1 January).

1960 Castro's government nationalises all US businesses in Cuba without compensation.

1961 CIA-trained Cuban exiles defeated at the Bay of Pigs.

1962 Cuban Missile Crisis.

1990 Russian trade and subsidies disappear; new austerity measures of the Special Period begin.

1993 Economic reforms begin, including acceptance of foreign investment and self-employment.

1994 Exodus of some 30,000 rafters to Florida; most are returned to Guantánamo Bay Naval Base.

1996 US passes Helms-Burton law forbidding US companies from doing business with Cuba.

2003 Worldwide criticism of Cuba's human rights record after imprisonment of 78 dissidents and execution of three hijackers.

2006 Fidel Castro temporarily hands power to his brother Raúl due to abdominal surgery.

2008 Fidel Castro announces that he will not stand for president; Raúl Castro is elected president.

WHERE TO GO

To the surprise of many first-time visitors, Cuba is no speck in the Caribbean. Nicolás Guillén, the nation's finest poet, described the island as a 'long green alligator'. Long it certainly is, at 1,250km (776 miles) from snout to tail. Nearly the size of England in terms of area, Cuba is divided into 14 provinces and incorporates some 450 offshore islands, known as *cayos* ('cays' or 'keys').

Given its size, you would need at least a month to explore Cuba fully. Most people begin their journeys in the capital, Havana, before heading to the prized tobacco lands further west and doubling back across the plains of sugar cane and some of the country's finest colonial towns in central Cuba. The eastern region, known as Oriente, has soaring mountains and Cuba's second and most musical city, Santiago de Cuba.

Resort hotels hug quintessential Caribbean beaches (mostly on the north coast). Although many package tourists still stick close to the coast, every region has charming, engaging towns. Sand and sun Cuba certainly has, but most visitors who dare to step away from the beach will find it simply too beguiling to spend a whole holiday lying idly in front of their hotels.

HAVANA (LA HABANA)

The island's capital, with almost 3 million inhabitants, is one of the most intoxicating cities in the world. Ever since its early maritime days and through the 1950s – when gangsters who ran prostitution and gambling rackets made Havana synonymous with decadence – it has always held a slightly seedy, languorous allure. That nostalgic appeal is still evident.

Backstreet in Trinidad, central Cuba

Today Havana is a one-of-a-kind, fascinating study in decay and rebirth. Unrestrained ocean waves and salty sea spray have wrecked huge chunks of the Malecón, the sumptuous promenade and roadway that traces the edge of the sea. Throughout the city, crumbling houses three and four storeys tall, somehow still standing, line backstreets where children play stickball and their parents and grandparents hover around doorstoops. In Old Havana, magnificently restored colonial palaces and stately baroque churches and convents crowd pulsating squares. Once the finest colonial city in the Americas, Havana's grandeur has not been destroyed even by decades of crisis and neglect. No less defiant than Fidel Castro himself, beneath the rubble this city is a living, breathing, vital and sensual creature.

Havana sprawls over more than 700 sq km (270 sq miles) and is divided into many districts. Those of greatest interest are Habana Vieja (Old Havana), Centro Habana (Central Havana), Vedado, and – to a lesser extent – Miramar. The latter two districts are newer residential and shopping barrios that extend west and south of the old city. While most areas within a neighbourhood can be covered comfortably on foot, passing from one to the other usually requires a taxi or *cocotaxi* (a buggy powered by a motorcycle engine).

Find that street

Cuban addresses usually include the street followed by a number. Helpful hints are also given: 'e/ …' ('between the streets …') or 'esq. …' ('corner of …').

Old Havana (La Habana Vieja)

The oldest section of Havana is the city's most spectacular, even if restoration work and gleaming coats of pastel colonial colours are leaving parts of it with a slightly more sanitised feel than the weathered working-class neighbourhoods that extend along the water and inland. As the location of

Colonial buildings in Old Havana

the city's greatest historical sites, **Old Havana** is where you'll want to spend most of your time, if it is limited.

First founded in 1515 on the south coast, Havana was moved to this site along a vast natural harbour in 1519. During the 16th century a fleet of galleons laden with treasures used the port as a pit stop on the way back to Spain from the New World. By the late 16th century, pirate attacks prompted the building of extensive city defences – colossal forts, a chain across the harbour mouth, and prominent city walls – making Havana the 'Bulwark of the West Indies'.

The wealthiest residents lived with their slaves in grand mansions constructed in the *mudéjar* style, a Christian-Muslim architectural tradition dating from the Spanish medieval period. Hidden courtyards bathed in penumbral light lurked behind massive doors, slatted blinds, carved iron window bars *(rejas)* and half-moon stained-glass windows *(mediopuntos)*.

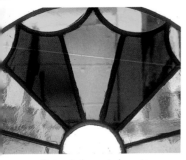

Stained-glass windows in Old Havana

The presence of such architectural wonders, no matter how dilapidated, led Unesco to add Old Havana (along with the city's early fortifications) to its World Heritage List in 1982. In the central tourist quarter, an expanding number of buildings are being spruced up, mainly with funds raised by the City Historian's Office, headed by Eusebio Leal Spengler. Once restored, the buildings are turned into hotels, museums and galleries, or become once more the splendid old shops they used to be. Many other buildings are propped up by wooden columns: their arcades, fluted pillars and mosaic tiles teetering on their last legs, awaiting their turn. At night, away from the main restaurant and bar areas, the darkness of the streets is punctuated only by the neon glow of television sets from tiny front rooms and the occasional headlights of gas-guzzling vintage Chevrolets and Plymouths, though much of the historical centre is now a pedestrians-only zone.

Havana's past lives on, evoked in part by legendary locations from the pages of popular novels and the lives of fiction writers. These include Graham Greene's **Hotel Sevilla**, where 'Our Man in Havana' went to meet his secret service contact, and Ernest Hemingway's favourite watering holes (El Floridita and La Bodeguita del Medio), as well as the **Hotel Ambos Mundos**, where he penned much of *For Whom the Bell Tolls*.

Old Havana is best experienced on foot, although you can also pick up a *cocotaxi* or *bicitaxi* to get to the Malecón or the museums at the district's edge.

Plaza de la Catedral

Havana's delicious **Plaza de la Catedral**, the focus of Habana Vieja life, could be a stage set. Tourists linger at El Patio's outdoor café, sipping mojitos and tapping their toes to Cuban *son*. The all-hours hubbub here is infectious. The glorious baroque façade and asymmetrical belltowers of the late 18th-century **cathedral** are the square's top attraction. The church, begun by Jesuits in 1748, is a thing of beauty; one half expects its bells to erupt in triumphant song. Its interior is surprisingly plain, but it once held the remains of Christopher Columbus. Just south of the cathedral are superb colonial mansions with bright shutters and *mediopuntos*, and an attractive little cul-de-sac (**Callejón de Chorro**) with a graphic arts workshop.

Of particular interest in the Cathedral Square is the **Museo de Arte Colonial** (San Ignacio 61 e/ Empedrado y O'Reilly; Wed–Sun 9.30am–7pm; charge) housed in the

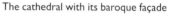

The cathedral with its baroque façade

Casa del Conde de Casa Bayona, a handsome palace dating to 1720. Its yellow courtyard and little-altered architectural features are complemented by a large collection of 17th- and 18th-century furniture.

Just round the corner, you'll find the atmospheric bar-restaurant **La Bodeguita del Medio** (Empedrado 207 e/ Cuba y San Ignacio; restaurant: noon–midnight, bar: 9am–midnight), which according to Hemingway served Havana's finest mojito (management apparently believes the notoriety is worth an extra two CUCs per drink). Like pilgrims to Ernest's drinking shrine, all tourists seem required to pay their respects here. Art exhibitions are held down the street at the **Centro de Arte Contemporáneo Wifredo Lam** (San Ignacio, 22 esq. Empedrado; Mon–Sat 9am–4.30pm; charge), named after Cuba's most famous 20th-century artist. Books, manuscripts and photographs of the country's best-known novelist are housed inside the **Fundación Alejo Carpentier** (Empedrado, 215; daily 8.30am–4.30pm; free).

Plaza de Armas

Plaza de Armas, which surrounds a statue of the patriot Céspedes and is ringed by shaded marble benches and second-hand bookstalls (Wed–Sat), is Havana's oldest square. It dates to the city's founding in 1519.

On the square's eastern side a small neoclassical temple, **El Templete**, marks the spot where the first Catholic mass was celebrated in 1519. Next door is one of the city's most luxurious hotels, Hotel Santa Isabel. To the north, the squat but angular and moated **Castillo de la Real Fuerza** (Fort of the Royal Forces; closed for renovation) is one of the oldest forts in the Americas, begun in 1558. The battlements afford views over the harbour, and the bronze *La Giraldilla* weather vane on one of the fort's towers – depicting a woman scanning the seas for her lost husband, an early Cuban governor – has been adopted as the symbol of the city and of Havana Club rum.

In 1791 the seat of government and the governor's (or captain general's) residence were transferred from the fort to the newly built, baroque **Palacio de los Capitanes Generales** on the square's western flank. A magnificent structure that was the presidential palace and then the municipal palace until Castro seized power, it now houses the **Museo de la Ciudad de la Habana** (Museum of the City of Havana; daily 9am–6pm; English-speaking guides; charge). Beyond the courtyard with a statue of Columbus lies a succession of splendid marbled and chandeliered rooms, some housing old cannonballs and coaches, others decked out with gilded furnishings. The most hallowed room commemorates Cuba's 19th-century independence wars, with the first Cuban flag and venerated personal objects from generals of the day.

Statue on Plaza de Armas

Calle Obispo

Running from Plaza de Armas to Parque Central, the pedestrianised **Calle Obispo** is Old Havana's most important thoroughfare. Here you

Casa de la Obra Pía

will find some smart shops catering to those with CUCs to spend, and you can peer into the courtyards of Havana's oldest homes. Equally fascinating are the two parallel, partly residential streets – O'Reilly and Obrapía – where neoclassical and colonial buildings intermingle with decrepit tenements. Restored Old Havana now extends all the way to Plaza Vieja and along pretty much all of Calle Obispo.

At no. 310 the **Museo Numismático** (e/ Aguiar y Habana; Tue–Sat 9.15am–4.45pm, Sun 9.l5am–1pm; charge) has a comprehensive set of Cuban coins and banknotes. Further east, on the corner of Mercaderes and Obispo, is the refurbished 1920s-era **Hotel Ambos Mundos**; Hemingway lived on and off in room 511 for a couple of years during the 1930s. The room is kept as it was during his time here. Those not staying in the hotel can visit the room for a small fee, or go to the rooftop bar for cocktails and views over Old Havana.

Nearby are several museums worth visiting as much for the glorious colonial mansions that house them as for their contents. The striking lemon-yellow **Casa de la Obra Pía** (Calle Obrapía, 158 e/ Mercaderes and San Ignacio; Tue–Sat 10.30am–4.30pm, Sun 9.30am–1pm; donations) is a 17th-century architectural wonder featuring baroque additions around a flower-drenched courtyard and a set of beautifully furnished domestic rooms. The owner, a member of one of Cuba's most important families, rescued orphan girls and took them into his home – an *obra pía* (work of piety) that lends its name to both the house and its street. The massive mansion opposite, nearly as impressive, houses the **Casa de África** (Tue–Sat 9am–5pm, Sun 9am–1pm; free), with pelts, drums, costumes, carved figures and furniture from some 26 African countries, as well as a tantalising collection of objects related to *santería*, the syncretic Afro-Cuban religion *(see below)* and various items related to Cuban slavery, such as manacles and traps.

On Calle Oficios at no. 16 lies the **Casa de los Árabes** (e/ Obispo y Obrapía; Tue–Sat 9am–5pm, Sun 9am–1pm; free), a Moorish-style 17th-century building that displays carpets,

Santería: The Cult of the Gods

Santería ('saint worship') is a syncretic religion derived from the Yoruba people in Nigeria and developed in Cuba by African slaves. Practitioners worship a complex pantheon of deities *(orishas)*, each with a specific character and a parallel Catholic saint – a guise that allowed slaves to disguise the religion from their hostile owners.

Initiates are chosen by a particular *orisha*, and they will wear the specific coloured beads of that saint and maintain shrines in their homes. The saints are believed to exercise control over almost every aspect of a person's life, but to communicate with them on matters of great importance, believers need the assistance of a *babalao* (priest), who will throw shells and perform other rituals to learn of the saints' commands. Saints' days are celebrations featuring Afro-Cuban drumming and dancing.

Many Cubans have at one time practised the rituals of santería – even Castro, allegedly. While difficult to quantify, its popularity appears to be increasing. In many parts of Cuba, one can see people wearing the coloured beads of their saint – red and white for Changó, the powerful god of war, and blue and white for Yemayá, the goddess of the sea – and others dressed all in white for initiation rights 'to become sainted'.

Part of the street furniture

robes and pottery, and contains Havana's only mosque (an ornate room upstairs). There's a lovely courtyard restaurant attached.

The streets of Havana are a living museum of chrome-finned wondercars imported during Detroit's heyday. Several that once belonged to pivotal Cuban figures – such as a 1918 Ford truck used by Fidel's father and Camilo Cienfuegos' Olds-mobile – are lined up in the **Museo de Automóviles** (Calle Oficios, 13 e/ Justiz y Obrapía; Tue–Sat 9am–4.30pm, Sun 9am–noon; charge).

Further south along Calle Oficios, is the splendidly restored Plaza de San Francisco, with upmarket restaurants and the imposing 18th-century **Convento de San Francisco de Asís** (daily 9am–6pm; charge). The convent contains a museum of religious treasures and a beautiful cloister. Concerts are frequently held here. Nearby, you'll find several impeccable colonial-era houses with brilliantly coloured façades.

Plaza Vieja

Follow charming and well-restored Calle Mercaderes to the fascinating and aptly named **Plaza Vieja** (Old Square), which was originally conceived in 1587 and housed wealthy merchants. It has received a massive facelift, with assistance from Unesco, and a neoclassical marble fountain gleams incongruously in the centre. In the southwest corner, a fine 18th-century palace, known as **La Casona**, has been converted into an arts centre; its balcony gives a lovely view of the plaza. In the northeastern corner, on the roof of a yellow-and-white wedding cake of a building, is the **Cámera Oscura** (Tue–Sat 9am–5.30pm, Sun 9am–1pm; charge), which gives up-close views of the city as well as wider vistas.

The old backstreets here are full of character. Down Calle Cuba, between Sol and Luz, stands the 17th-century **Convento de Santa Clara** (Mon–Fri 8am–5pm; charge), an expansive complex that takes up four small blocks. Inside is a tranquil courtyard garden full of exotic trees. A convent until 1919, it is now an architectural conservation centre. It is also a hostel, Residencia Académica Santa Clara, which provides peaceful, simple rooms, used mainly by student groups.

By the railway station, between Calles Picota and Egido, is **Casa Natal de José Martí** (at Calle Leonor Pérez, 314; Tue–Sat 9am–5pm; charge), the modest birthplace of poet

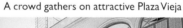

A crowd gathers on attractive Plaza Vieja

and statesman José Martí. The numerous personal effects on display here leave no doubt about the fact that Martí is Cuba's pre-eminent national hero.

Capitolio

Calle Brasil (also called Teniente Rey) leads directly west from Plaza Vieja to the monumental **Capitolio** (tours daily 9am–7pm; charge), a replica of the American capitol in Washington, DC. Completed in 1929, it reflects the period when Cuba was in the thrall of the United States. Its vast bronze doors pictorially chart the island's history, and the immense main gallery inside has a replica diamond in the floor beneath the dome, that marks the spot from which all distances in the country are measured.

The Capitolio Nacional

Directly behind the Capitolio is the **Partagás Tobacco Factory** (Industria, 520 e/ Dragones y Barcelona; Mon–Fri; tours start every 15 mins, 9–11am and noon–3pm; no photos; charge), the biggest export factory in the country – with more than 200 rollers churning out 5 million cigars a year – and one of Havana's top tourist draws. This factory, which has been rolling out *puros* since the mid-19th century, is the best (and, with a charge of CUC$10, the most expensive) to visit on the island; it also has a fine tobacco shop and smoking lounge for *aficionados* and wannabes. If the cigars inside strike you as too expensive, you'll have plenty of opportunity to purchase fake or stolen stogies outside the factory, as every third person whispers 'You want cigar?' as you pass. Bear in mind that customs regulations are tight: you're allowed to take home only

The Partagás factory

23 individual cigars without official receipt, and fakes (as well as being inferior) are likely to be confiscated.

Just east of the Capitolio, on Parque Central near the classic Hotel Inglaterra, stands the magnificent **Gran Teatro de la Habana**, built in 1837. The home of the Cuban National Ballet and Opera drips with ornate balustrades, shutters and sculpted columns. The cavernous interior is hardly less awesome but can only be visited during performances.

Those with the Hemingway bug can visit **El Floridita**, at the intersection of Calles Obispo and Montserrate, one block east of Parque Central. The writer immortalised the swanky bar in *Islands in the Stream*. A bronze statue of Papa now leans against the bar, his photos adorn the walls, and his favourite daiquiri is now referred to as the 'Papa Hemingway', with double rum and no sugar (everyone knows he was an alcoholic; barmen claim he was also diabetic). At CUC$6 a daiquiri, the place is a bit of a tourist trap, but still capable of evoking the kind of hedonistic refuge expat writers adored.

On the same side of the Parque Central is the **Museo Nacional Palacio de Bellas Arts** (Tue–Sat 10am–6pm, Sun 10am–2pm; charge, combined ticket available with the Arte

Colourful buildings on the Prado

Cubano collection). Many of the paintings were left behind by ruling-class families who fled Cuba in 1959. This building contains the Arte Universal collection, while a few blocks northeast on Trocadero is the **Museo Nacional de Arte Cubano**, an excellent collection housed in the 1954 Fine Arts Palace. This showcase gallery was opened by Castro in 2001 after a five-year refurbishment.

Another few blocks northeast, housed in the grand presidential palace used by presidents (and dictators) between 1920 and 1959, is the **Museo de la Revolución** (daily 10am–5pm; English-speaking guides; charge), Cuba's largest and most fascinating museum. Allow a couple of hours to see this exhaustive exhibition of the trajectory of the 1959 Cuban Revolution. The most absorbing sections chart the struggle to power with countless maps, evocative photos of both torture victims and triumphal scenes, and assorted personal memorabilia from passports and worn-out shoes to Kalashnikov rifles and bloodstained clothes. In the square outside is the *Granma*, the boat that carried Castro and his 81 rebels from Mexico to Cuba in 1956; it is now enclosed in glass, guarded by military police and surrounded by other revolutionary relics, such as a tractor converted into a tank and the delivery van used in the failed attack on the Presidential Palace in 1957.

The Prado

West of the oldest sections and intimate streets of Old Havana is an area of wide boulevards and grand palaces. The loveliest avenue, the **Prado** (officially known as Paseo de Martí), runs from Parque Central to the sea. Grand but rundown buildings, with fading flamingo-pink and lime-green façades, and ornate columns, flank a raised promenade of laurels, gas lamps and marble benches. In the 19th century this was the most fashionable strolling ground for the city's wealthy. Now it serves as a minipark for *habaneros*, from musicians and roaming couples to children playing on homemade skateboards and go-karts, or practising baseball shots.

On the seafront (1 Capdevilla) the **Museo Nacional de la Música** (National Museum of Music; Tue–Sat 10am–6pm, Sun 9am–noon; charge) is of interest mainly for its extensive, informative collection of African drums and the many stringed instruments used in Cuban traditional music.

Havana's Forts

Cuba's most impressive forts sit brooding over the capital's commercial harbour. Take a taxi through the road tunnel beneath the water to reach them. The older one, built at the end of the 16th century, is the **Castillo de los Tres Santos Reyes Magos del Morro**, better known as 'El Morro'. From its position at the harbour mouth, the views of Havana over the defiant cannons are magical.

The vast **Fortaleza de San Carlos de la Cabaña** (known as 'La Cabaña'), running beside the harbour, was constructed after the English capture of Havana in 1763. The largest fort ever built in the Americas, it is impressively well preserved, and the gardens and ramparts are romantically lit in the evening. A ceremony held at 9pm (El Cañonazo) re-enacts the firing of a cannon that marked the closing of the city gates.

New Havana

The walls surrounding Old Havana were razed during the 19th century to allow the city to expand westwards. The long, curvaceous and crumbling **Malecón** (breakwater), a six-lane highway alongside the city's north shore, links the districts of Central Havana and Vedado. The victim of harmful salt spray, the seafront drive is now more a seafront dive. At its eastern end, primary-coloured buildings – a showcase of tragic splendour – seem to fall apart before your eyes. Havana's youth congregate along the Malecón on fine evenings, flying kites, canoodling, swimming off the rocks, and setting out to sea in giant inner tubes to fish.

Smiles along the Malecón

Although most visitors will want to concentrate on historic Old Havana, the newer districts provide a fascinating view of the areas where most people live and work. The most interesting districts of **New Havana** are Central Havana and Vedado. The former is a congested, lower-middle-class *barrio* (neighbourhood) with few attractions, although a walk along its dusty streets can be an eye-opening experience. Vedado is the city's principal commercial and residential zone – the epicentre of middle-class Havana – with parks, monuments, hotels, restaurants, theatres and the University of Havana. Once the stomping grounds of the elite in the 1950s, the 'suburb' of Miramar today is home to foreign companies investing in Cuba and numerous diplomatic missions of foreign governments.

Central Havana
Central Havana (Centro Habana) is a ramshackle residential and commercial area. The city's main shopping

Dancer on Callejón Hamel

street, **Calle San Rafael**, traverses it from the Parque Central westwards. This might be Havana at its least guarded. You can stop to have your nails painted, or get a shave and a haircut, all right on the pavement. One of the country's new private markets has over-run Havana's small **China-town**, at Calles Zanja and Rayo. A few Chinese restaurants selling Cuban-Oriental food are all that remain of what was once the largest Chinatown in Latin America in the 1950s.

The neighbourhood of **Cayo Hueso**, just behind the Malecón, is a rough-and-tumble *barrio* once populated by cigar-factory workers. Today the main reason to visit is to see **Callejón Hamel**, where the artist Salvador González has dedicated himself to preserving the area's Afro-Cuban culture. The small alleyway is entirely done over in street art, sculptures and murals. González's studio is here, and on Sunday at noon–3pm there are performances of Afro-Cuban ritual and rumba.

Vedado

Vedado is a respectable business district as well as a leafy residential area, spacious and orderly in comparison with Old and Central Havana. It had its heyday in the 1940s and 1950s, when such gangsters as Meyer Lansky held sway in the Nacional, Riviera and Capri hotels. Stars like Frank Sinatra and Ginger Rogers performed, and American tourists emptied their wallets in glittering casinos. The Revolution put the lid on the nightlife by banning gambling and deporting the Mafiosi. Today, new or refurbished hotels of international standard welcome travellers on business or for pleasure.

Business is centred on **La Rampa**, the name for Calle 23 from Calle L to the sea. Opposite the tower-block Hotel Habana Libre – the Havana Hilton in pre-revolutionary days – is the **Coppelia ice cream park**. At this institution, locals queue for hours for the prized ice cream, eating several scoops in one sitting or ladling them into saucepans to take home. Foreigners can join the queue as well; payment is in *moneda nacional*. Coppelia was instrumental in the award-winning Cuban film *Fresa y Chocolate* ('Strawberry and Chocolate'), a daring film when it came out in 1994 which dealt with freedoms, homosexuality and revolutionary fervour in contemporary Havana (its title is a wry reference to the lack of choices of ice cream flavours – indeed, of all things – in Cuba).

Hotel Nacional in Vedado

A short walk up the hill brings you to the University of Havana, founded in the early 18th century, a quiet, attractive campus of neoclassical buildings. English-speaking students eager to meet foreigners are numerous here.

Directly east on Calle San Miguel, 1159 between

Calles Ronda and Mazón is the **Museo Napoleónico** (Tue–Sat 9am–4.30pm, Sun 9am–12.30pm; charge). The mansion holds not only Empire furniture but also a remarkable collection of Napoleonic memorabilia: portraits, busts and even his pistol, hat and a cast of his death mask from St Helena. The house and contents were appropriated by the state from a rich owner in 1960.

In the same year, the government acquired the **Museo de Artes Decorativas** (Tue–Sat 10.30am–5.30pm, Sun 9.30am–noon; charge), at Calle 17, 502 between Calles D and E. Each room in this grand 19th-century villa is furnished in a particular style: English Chippendale, Chinese, baroque, or Art Deco in the fabulous bathroom.

The iron sculpture of Che on Plaza de la Revolución

Massive marble mausoleums line the principal avenues of the **Cementerio de Cristóbal Colón** (Columbus Cemetery; entrance on Zapata y 12; daily 9am–5pm; English speaking guides; charge), which is a vast city of the dead established in the late 19th century. Cubans come here to pray and place flowers at the tomb of La Milagrosa ('The Miracle Worker'), who helps people in need. It is said that she was buried with her infant at her feet, but when their bodies were exhumed, the child was cradled in her arms.

Plaza de la Revolución

The **Plaza de la Revolución** is a vast, stark concourse where political rallies are held; otherwise it is usually empty. The square is dominated by grim high-rise ministry buildings, erected in the 1950s by Batista, and the **José Martí Memorial** – a giant, tapering obelisk that looks like a rocket launch pad – with a pensive marble statue of Cuba's greatest hero and a **museum** about his life (Mon–Sat 9am–5pm; charge). The obelisk's lookout gives superb panoramic views. Adorning the Ministry of the Interior building opposite is a giant iron sculpture-mural of Che, illuminated at night.

Miramar

To the west is the exclusive district of **Miramar**. The villas of the pre-revolutionary rich, expropriated by the state, have now been turned into apartments or offices. But embassies along Avenida 5 still imbue the area with a privileged feel.

At the corner of Calle 14, the **Museo del Ministerio del Interior** (Tue–Fri 9am–5pm, Sat 9am–4pm; charge) has some intriguing exhibits relating to CIA espionage, including code boxes concealed in briefcases, decoding equipment, a transmitter hidden in a fake rock, and a range of explosive devices. Don't miss the Russian Embassy, between Calles 62 and 66, which looks like a giant concrete robot.

Growing as an attraction – literally – the **Maqueta de la Habana** (Calle 28, 113 e/ Avenida 1 y 3; Mon–Sat 9.30am–5pm; charge) is a scale model of the city in astounding 1:1,000 detail. A visit to the Maqueta can help organise the city's neighbourhoods in your mind.

Casa de la Música

The Casa de la Música in Miramar is one of the best shows in town. This is where Cubans come to dance their hearts out to salsa and other rhythms played by live bands. And foreigners join in too.

Casa de Ernest Hemingway

Havana's Outskirts

Havana's sprawling suburbs contain a couple of places associated with Ernest Hemingway that are magnets for those seeking to trace the author's life in Cuba. From 1939 to 1960 he lived on and off in the **Finca La Vigía**, now the **Casa Museo de Ernest Hemingway** (Wed–Mon 9am–4.30pm; charge). The house (under renovation) is 11km (7 miles) southeast of Havana in San Francisco de Paula, so you will have to take a taxi. Visitors may not enter the graceful villa, but by peering through windows you can see all the rooms furnished as the writer had them, covered in bullfighting posters and filled with more than 9,000 books, including such titles as *The Guide to Hunting and Fishing in Cuba.* You can roam the lush gardens searching out his motorboat, the *Pilar*, and the swimming pool where Ava Gardner once skinny-dipped.

Hemingway kept the *Pilar* 10km (6 miles) east of Havana at **Cojímar**. Next to the little fort is a Hemingway bust, looking out over the bay. The writer frequented La Terraza restaurant nearby *(see page 139)*, worth visiting for its many photographs of Hemingway. His captain and cook aboard the *Pilar* was the fisherman Gregorio Fuentes. Until his death at the age of 104 in 2002, Gregorio would regale visitors with tales of his hero. He always denied that he was Santiago, the title character in *The Old Man and the Sea*, but he did not dispute that it was in Cojímar that Hemingway found the inspiration for his famous novel.

Approximately 18km (11 miles) east of Havana (20 minutes' drive), the long, sandy **Playas del Este** (Eastern Beaches) are a big draw for Cubans. They are the closest beaches to the capital and particularly lively on Sundays.

Ernie and Graham: Literary Footprints

Ernest Hemingway's literary and personal footprints are as deep in Cuba as they are in Spain, and they've become part of the tourist fabric in both places. Hemingway wrote two books based in Cuba, *The Old Man and The Sea* and *Islands in the Stream*, and in large part he wrote *For Whom the Bell Tolls* (about the Spanish Civil War) from his hotel room in Havana. He was an island resident for two decades. Pilgrims can trace his life in Cuba at various sights, including Finca La Vigía, Cojímar, El Floridita, La Bodeguita del Medio and the Hotel Ambos Mundos. Despite chummy photos with Castro (they met at the annual Hemingway Fishing Tournament, which Fidel won), the writer's views on the Revolution are elusive, although all Cubans accept him as a fervent supporter. His views notwithstanding, it is certain that he identified with the Cuban people. Hemingway abandoned Cuba in 1960 and committed suicide shortly thereafter in Idaho.

Graham Greene's classic novel about Cuban intrigue, *Our Man in Havana*, was first published in 1958. Not only is it an evocative portrait of sleazy 1950s Havana, with scenes set in the Nacional and Sevilla hotels and the Tropicana nightclub. It's also eerily prescient, as the hero invents drawings of Soviet weapons hidden in the Cuban countryside, long before Castro aligned the country with the USSR. Greene was a great supporter of the Revolution, praising Castro, the war against illiteracy, the lack of racial segregation, and the support of the arts. When he went to Cuba to do research for the book in 1958, he took supplies for Castro, who was secluded in the Sierra Maestra, in exchange for an interview that never took place. Greene's support wavered, though, when he learned of the Revolution's forced labour camps in the 1960s.

PINAR DEL RÍO PROVINCE

Due west of Havana is **Pinar del Río province**, Cuba's westernmost region – a finger of land with the Gulf of Mexico to the north and the Caribbean to the south. It contains some of Cuba's most beautiful countryside among the lush Guaniguanico mountains and surrounding patchwork of verdant fields *(vegas)*, where the world's finest tobacco is cultivated. In the beautiful Viñales Valley, tobacco fields and ancient limestone formations produce spectacular scenery more reminiscent of Southeast Asia than the Caribbean. In this resolutely agricultural region, oxen pulling ploughs that till the red-earth fields and cowboy farmers *(guajiros)* on horseback are much more common than cars. Residents of Havana might think of it as a poor backwater, but the easy, almost somnolent pace, breathtaking countryside, and welcoming residents of Pinar del Río make it one of Cuba's certain highlights.

There are beaches and excellent diving further west, near **Playa María la Gorda**, but for most visitors the star attractions are the irresistible little town of Viñales and its beautiful valley. Many visitors take organised daytrips to the region from Havana hotels, but an overnight stay in Viñales – overlooking the valley – is highly recommended.

Start your explorations by driving west on the *autopista* (highway) linking Havana with the province's capital city of Pinar del Río. About 63km (39 miles) along the highway, a turnoff leaves the level, palm-dotted plains for **Soroa**, where a richly endowed botanical garden nestles in the mountain foothills near a tourist complex. A guided tour reveals an orchid garden, lychee and mango trees, coffee plants and splendid specimens of *jagüey* and *ceiba* trees. A restaurant in the villa of Castillo de las Nubes on a nearby mountain has stunning views.

The Viñales Valley with its distinctive *mogotes*

Pinar del Río

At the end of the highway, 175km (109 miles) west of Havana, the small city of **Pinar del Río** is a bustling commercial centre. Along the main street, Calle José Martí, low-rise neoclassical buildings in blues, yellows, greens and orange have a stately but dilapidated quality. You'll find a small, touristy tobacco factory, **Francisco Donatien Fábrica de Tabacos** (Maceo 157; Mon–Sat 8am–5pm; charge), housed in an old jail below the Plaza de la Independencia. Visitors are welcome here and at the less picturesque **Casa Garay Rum Factory** (Mon–Sat 8am–5pm; charge), on Avenida Isabel Rubio, where they make a local rum liqueur called *guayabita del Pinar*.

The road southwest from the city to San Juan y Martínez leads deep into tobacco's heartland – the **Vuelta Abajo** – where the world's greatest tobacco is grown. Amid fields of big green leaves ripening in the sun and plantations covered in white gauze sheets stand steep-roofed barns where leaves are hung on poles with a needle and thread and then dried, turning from green to brown.

Some 27km (17 miles) to the north of Pinar del Río lies the most picturesque corner of Cuba. The deeply green **Viñales Valley** is spattered with *mogotes*, sheer-sided limestone masses covered in thick vegetation. These are the remnants of a collapsed cavern system that was created underwater at least 150 million years ago, in the Jurassic period. Tobacco (of slightly lesser quality than in the Vuelta Abajo) grows here in a patchwork of fields and dries in *bohíos*, constructed with shaggy thatch. Cigar-chomping *guajiros* in huge straw hats urge on their oxen, as vultures swoop overhead. At any time of day you can wander the fields and meet the farmers, who might even offer you a cigar.

Tobacco drying

At **Casa del Veguero** (Carretera a Viñales, km 25) you'll find the grizzled farmer Celestibo Alvarez, 'El Niño', whom the government has unofficially appointed as the face of tobacco – Cuba's Marlboro man. Next to his farm, on the road into Viñales, is a state-owned tobacco and souvenir shop. The best valley views can be had from either of its lovely hotels: Los Jazmines and Horizontes La Ermita *(see pages 130–1)*. The sight at dusk is especially alluring.

Viñales

The little town of **Viñales** is surprisingly spruce, with a fetching, arcaded main street and lovely rustic scenes along the back lanes. Near the Cupet petrol station as you leave town heading north towards Puerto de Esperanza, is the delightful **Jardín Botánico** overseen by two elderly women and their brother, whose parents began planting the hundreds of species of plants in the 1930s. A guide will show you around the fruit trees

Homo sapiens at the Mural de la Prehistoria

and flowers and let you taste the produce (tip appreciated).

Nearby a couple of local tourist sights, on all the package excursions, have curiosity value but not much else. One limestone *mogote* just west of town was painted by local artists dangling on ropes in the 1960s with a **Mural de la Prehistoria** (Mural of Prehistory) – commissioned by Castro himself – that is 120m (370ft) high and 180m (550ft) long. The garish painting, an exercise in bad judgment and sloppy execution, depicts evolution from an ammonite to a dinosaur to advanced (and presumably socialist) *Homo sapiens*. All the creatures depicted were indigenous to the area. Eight kilometres (5 miles) to the north of town, the extensive **Cueva del Indio** (Indian Cave) was used as a hideout by Indians after the conquest. A tour through the cave includes a brief ride on an underground river in a boat (which would-be emigrants once stole for an unsuccessful escape attempt to Florida). Both mural and cave have tourist restaurants.

Islands North & South

Just off the province's north and south coasts are three contrasting islands. To the north, **Cayo Levisa** is a small coral cay, about 3km (1¼ miles) long and just several hundred metres wide at most points, which has pristine beaches, clear waters and coral reefs. The island is a half-hour ferry ride from Palma Rubia (ferries leave at 10am and 5.30pm). There's a well-equipped diving centre, and overnight accommodation is available in the simple Villa Cayo Levisa bungalow complex, which has a restaurant and a bar.

Cayo Levisa

On the other side of Cuba, stretching eastwards from Pinar del Río's southern coast, is the Archipiélago de los Canarreos. There are two main islands. **Cayo Largo**, 25km (15½ miles) long and the most easterly of the archipiélago, might be your Caribbean paradise – if all you're looking for is a dazzling white beach and clear blue seas. Other than the kilometres of beaches, there's not much else of consequence here except mangrove, scrub and half a dozen comfortable all-inclusive hotels with a full programme of entertainment and watersports. Turtles nest in the sand at one end of the island. At the other you can go sailing, diving and deep-sea fishing or take a boat trip to **Playa Sirena**, an incomparable strip of sand a 10-minute boat ride away, where lobster lunches are available.

Cayo Largo, with its captive tourist audience, is considerably more expensive than the mainland. Some package tourists spend the whole of their holiday on Cayo Largo. Those with low boredom thresholds might consider coming for the day or perhaps staying overnight, taking the half-hour flights from Havana and Varadero.

By contrast, the **Isla de la Juventud** (Isle of Youth) sees few tourists except those at the rather isolated Hotel El Colony (on the Siguanea Bay, half way along the island's western shore), who come exclusively for the superb diving off the island's southwestern tip. Cuba's largest offshore island, some 50km (31 miles) in diameter, the Isle of Youth is not its prettiest. It is said to have been the location for Robert Louis Stevenson's *Treasure Island*; pirates once buried their booty here. The island received its jaunty name in the 1970s, when as many as 22,000 foreign students (mainly from politically sympathetic African countries) studied here in no fewer than 60 schools.

The island fails to live up to its colourful past. The number of foreign students has dropped to fewer than 5,000, and derelict boarding schools dot the monotonous countryside. However, there are plenty of virgin beaches to be discovered, and in a cave at **Punta del Este** you can examine enigmatic symbols painted centuries ago by Ciboney Indians.

For more accessible entertainment, **Nueva Gerona**, the island's little capital, is moderately attractive, with striped awnings along its smart, pillared main street.

Presidio Modelo

Just east of Nueva Gerona is the fascinating Presidio Modelo (Tue–Sat 9am–4.30pm, Sun 9am–1pm; charge). The dictator Machado built this copy of a US penitentiary in 1931. Castro and 26 of his rebels were sent here after the storming of the Moncada Barracks; their ward and Castro's solitary confinement cell have been restored.

MATANZAS PROVINCE

The province east of Havana – largely flat sugar-cane country – was in the 19th century Cuba's most important cane-producing region. For today's visitors, however, the focus is on the beach resort of Varadero, Cuba's biggest draw, with opportunities for side trips to atmospheric, time-warped towns and to the swamplands of the south coast.

Varadero

Varadero has enthusiastic proponents and equally passionate detractors among its visitors. A long peninsula with many dozens of hotels and restaurants, bars, fast-food cafés and grocery shops stretching right to the tip (and more of each on the way), Varadero doesn't feel much like Cuba at all. It is a package tourist enclave, and plenty of visitors fly into it and never leave. If you want to see and learn what makes Cuba a fascinating place, though, you'll need to escape for at least a couple of daytrips. In towns around Cuba you'll meet tourists who – like jailbird escapees – rejoice at having got out of Varadero.

Still, there are plenty of delighted people for whom this is heaven: a 20km (12-mile) long, virtually uninterrupted white-sand beach with shallow, clean waters. Varadero isn't a recent development by a government desperate for hard currency (though officials are determined to see it become a faceless cash cow not unlike Cancún). It was in the 1920s that Varadero first attracted millionaires, who built palatial holiday villas. They were led by Alfred Irenée Dupont who bought up most of the peninsula and used to live at the opulent beachside **Mansion Xanadú**, which he had built in 1930 and which is now an exclusive six-room hotel. Tourism proper began after World War II with the construction of casinos and such establishments as the Hotel Internacional.

Even the beach, Varadero's best feature, can be problematic. Northern winds kick up with considerable frequency, and life-guards put out the red flags to warn of the dangerous under-tow. There is often a strong smell from the oil pumps on the resort's outskirts. Prostitution and hassling are much less of a problem than they once were, after a crackdown in 1999, but other pests (namely mosquitoes) can be a real annoyance. Moreover, the resort is spread out over 17km (11 miles), with no real centre, so you need transport to get around.

On the other hand, Varadero has many extremely com-fortable hotels (most of them the results of international joint ventures), open bars and an excellent range of watersports. And, unlike other parts of Cuba, topless sunbathing is allowed here. If you tire of the beach, there are organised excursions to every conceivable point of interest on the island – including Havana.

Souvenir sellers at Varadero

Varadero occupies a long, thin insular spit of sand, with water on both sides and a bridge to the mainland. Between Calles 25 and 54 there's something of a local community of Cubans, with ancient Cadillacs parked outside rickety wooden bungalows. The liveliest area is around Calles 54 to 64, with a shopping mall, a host of restaurants and bars, and the **Retiro Josone**, a pretty park set around a palm-fringed boating lake.

Spreading several kilometres further east are the newest hotel complexes and an 18-hole golf course at Xanadú.

Matanzas and Cárdenas

Though just spitting distance away, these quintessentially Cuban towns are a world apart from Varadero. Their poorly stocked shops, dusty backstreets and primitive transport provide Varadero's package tourists with a convenient insight into Cuban life before they're whisked back to their hotels.

Matanzas, 42km (26 miles) west of Varadero, is busy and grimy. Lying alongside a deep bay, it came into its own during the 19th century as the country's sugar capital. On the leafy main square, Parque Libertad, the **Museo Farmacéutico** (Mon–Fri 10am–6pm, Sun 8am–noon; charge) is a wonderfully preserved chemist's shop, founded in 1882. On a street running east towards the bay, the **Catedral de San Carlos Borromeo** is notable for its many murals.

A little further to the east, impressive buildings on Plaza de la Vigía include the **Palacio de Junco**, which houses a second-rate provincial museum, and the **Teatro Sauto**. Constructed in 1863, the lovely theatre has tiers of wrought-iron boxes and a mural ceiling; there are performances most weekends.

Las Cuevas de Bellamar (Tue–Sun 9am–6pm; charge), a short distance east, are Cuba's oldest tourist attraction. The caves were discovered by chance in 1861 by a Chinese slave. Tours (in English) take you down into a vast chamber for views of the many stalactites and stalagmites.

Mangroves near Playa Larga on the Zapata Peninsula

Fortunes have changed for the town of **Cárdenas**, 15km (9 miles) east of Varadero. Once the island's most important sugar-exporting port, it's now a somewhat ramshackle place. But the main square is elegant, and the **Museo Oscar María de Rojas** (Avenida 4/Calle 12), the second oldest museum in the country, houses a quirky collection of items. There is also the **Museo de la Batalla de Ideas** (Tue–Sat 9am–5pm; charge). Inaugurated by Castro in 2001, it documents the campaign for the repatriation of Elián, a local boy who was at the centre of international controversy in 1999–2000. His mother died while fleeing with him to Miami, but after months of heated controversy he was returned by the US authorities to live with his father.

Zapata Peninsula

The **Zapata Peninsula** is the largest wetland area in the Caribbean, flat as a pancake and covered in mangrove swamps and grassland plains. Its protected wildlife includes crocodiles, manatees and numerous species of birds. Frankly, though, you are unlikely to see any interesting wildlife unless you take a guided bird-watching trip from **Playa Larga**. You can see penned reptiles at the crocodile farm at **La Boca**, a popular tourist site where you can pose with a baby croc and taste crocodile steak.

A more appealing prospect is picturesque **Guamá**, a half-hour boat ride from La Boca along an artificial channel and then across the vast **Laguna del Tesoro** (Treasure Lake). Legend has it that the Indians dumped their jewels into the water rather than surrender them to Spanish *conquistadores*. Guamá is a group of tiny islands connected by wooden bridges. A few visitors stay in the thatched *cabañas (see page 132)*, but most just come to wander along the boardwalk, greet the ducks and egrets, and have a meal.

Battle beach

'Playa Girón: La Primera Derrota del Imperialismo en América Latina' ('The First Defeat of Imperialism in Latin America') – billboard at Bay of Pigs.

It may be peaceful now, but the Zapata Peninsula is best known for the violence and bloodshed that once visited its shores. South of La Boca you soon come to Playa Girón – site of the 1961 US-led **Bay of Pigs** invasion *(see page 19)*, in which more than 100 people were killed. At irregular intervals along the often crab-infested road are a number of concrete memorials to those who died during the invasion. There are two simple, isolated bungalow hotel complexes on the bay, one at quiet **Playa Larga**, the other at **Playa Girón**, where the already scruffy beach is further spoiled by a concrete breakwater. One major attraction, however, is the excellent **Museo Playa Girón** (daily 9am–5pm; charge) which serves as an emotional memorial to the three-day Bay of Pigs debacle.

Trinidad and the Sierra del Escambray

CENTRAL CUBA

Tourists usually whiz through central Cuba. The only tourist beacons are on or near the coasts: in the south around Cienfuegos and at Trinidad, and in the north at Cayo Coco and Guillermo and Playa Santa Lucía. But there is much else to see.

Central Cuba comprises five provinces: Cienfuegos, Villa Clara, Sancti Spíritus, Ciego de Avila and Camagüey. Each focuses on a provincial city of the same or similar name, typically of some interest yet not likely to detain you for longer than a day. The west has the best scenery, in the Sierra del Escambray mountains. To the east of Sancti Spíritus, towns lie on flat plains. This used to be the main sugar cane growing area in the 1970s, but the collapse of the sugar-for-oil trade with the USSR in the 1990s led to the closure of many sugar factories. In Camagüey, the cattle-ranch province, watermills punctuate the skyline and *vaqueros* (cowboys) slouch on horses.

Cienfuegos

The best feature of the port city of **Cienfuegos** (250km/155 miles southeast of Havana) is its position, set at the back of a large bay. Despite the industry on its periphery, the centre is quite attractive, with pastel-coloured neoclassical buildings. Many travellers now stop off here on their way to Trinidad.

The focal point in town is **Parque José Martí**, one of the grandest squares in the country. Here you will find the monumental red-domed government offices, an early 19th-century cathedral with a startling gold-painted interior, and a music hall (*casa de la trova*) with whimsical flourishes. Take a guided tour of the town's finest colonial building, the **Teatro Tomás Terry**, on the north side of the square. Built in 1890, it was named after a rich sugar plantation owner from Venezuela. The interior, largely original, has a lovely frescoed ceiling and a semicircle of tiered boxes and wooden seats. Enrico Caruso and Sara Bernhardt once performed here, and on weekends you may be able to catch a performance by one of Cuba's top ballet companies. The **Catedral de la Purísima Concepción**, built in 1870, is on the east side of the square. It has an attractive interior with stained-glass windows depicting the 12 apostles.

The Prado is the town's principal thoroughfare, a palm-lined boulevard that takes you down to the spit of land protruding into the bay past smart waterside villas. At the edge of Punta Gorda, near the end of the Malecón (Calle 37), is the **Palacio de Valle**. This

Botanical highlight

The Jardín Botánico Soledad (daily 8am–5pm; charge), 23km (14 miles) outside Cienfuegos at Pepito Tey on the road to Trinidad, is the oldest botanical garden in Cuba (it dates from 1899) and one of the best tropical gardens in the world. Cubatur or Havanatur In Cienfuegos can arrange guided tours; alternatively, go straight there and join a tour at the entrance.

ornate palace, now a restaurant, was finished in 1917; its ceilings and walls are covered in patterned stonework.

At the mouth of the bay, on the western side, the **Castillo de Jagua** (Mon–Sat 9am–5pm, Sun 9am–1pm; charge) was constructed by the Spanish in 1732 (long before the city's founding in 1819) to ward off pirates. You reach the castle on a tiny ferry from

Teatro Tomás Terry, Cienfuegos

the Hotel Pasacaballo on the eastern side of the bay. Close to the hotel is the best beach in the area, **Playa Rancho Luna**.

Trinidad

The scenic, undulating 80km (50-mile) road east from Cienfuegos to Trinidad skirts the foothills of the Sierra del Escambray, Cuba's second-highest mountain range. The beguiling town of **Trinidad**, the third of Diego Velázquez's original seven settlements, subsequently became rich through the smuggling, slave and sugar trades. Its sizable old town is endowed with marvellous Spanish colonial architecture and has been named by Unesco as a World Heritage Site. Cuba could package it as a time capsule: it is the island's prettiest town and one of the finest preserved colonial cities in all the Americas. There's been a preservation order on Trinidad since the 1950s.

Within easy striking distance of Trinidad are enough attractions to make a longer stay especially rewarding, including the fine beach of Playa Ancón, the lush Valle de los Ingenios (Valley of the Sugar Mills), and waterfalls and treks in the Escambray mountains.

Restored mansions of the well-to-do have been turned into museums, while art galleries, craft shops and restaurants occupy additional lovely old buildings. No traffic, not even bicycles, can cope well with Trinidad's wildly uneven, cobbled street surfaces, so it's a fairly peaceful place, though the calm at night has been disturbed somewhat by the arrival of live music venues in the centre. But these are fun, and it's still a pleasant, relaxed place. If you spend a night here you can experience the town without the tour-bus hordes.

The old town clusters around the **Plaza Mayor**, a delightful square of painted railings, fanciful urns, greyhound statues and colonial buildings. To the left of the relatively plain church, Iglesia de la Santísima Trinidad, is the **Museo Romántico** (Tue–Sun 9am–5pm; charge) with a collections of fine furniture and porcelain. The square's two other museums both have attractive courtyards and cool interiors. The **Museo de Arqueología Guamuhaya** (Tue–Sat 9am–5pm; charge) exhibits bones of indigenous tribespeople and slaves. The **Museo de Arquitectura Colonial** (Mon–Thur and Sat 9am–5pm, Sun 9am–1pm; charge) has examples of woodwork, ironwork, stained glass and other items culled from colonial houses.

A block to the north of the Plaza Mayor in a former con-

Trinidad's Plaza Mayor

vent is the **Museo Nacional de Lucha Contra Bandidos** (National Museum of the Struggle against Counter-Revolutionaries; Tue–Sat 9am–5pm, Sun 9am–1pm; charge), which documents the campaign to weed out rebels who hid in the Escambray mountains in the 1960s. The 360-degree view from the yellow belltower is the big draw.

Transport in Trinidad

A block south of Plaza Mayor on Calle Simón Bolívar stands the grand Palacio Cantero, built in 1830. Painted pillars, scrolls, shells, pediments and drapes embellish the interior, eclipsing the historical artefacts and old furniture that now form the **Museo Municipal de Historia** (Sat–Thur 9am–5pm; charge). It has its own fine tower, though climbing its rickety narrow steps can be a trial if a group has arrived there first.

It might be possible to take a peek inside the tiny **Piro Guinart cigar factory** (on Maceo at the corner of Colón), which employs only about 30 hand rollers. A block south of the Plaza Mayor are two streets completely given over to sellers of handmade lace and other crafts. Further afield, southeast along Calle José Mendoza, you'll find the evocative ruins of **Iglesia de Santa Ana**, and overlooking the town from the north is the **Ermita La Papa**, a bricked-up church, on a hill where boys fly homemade kites.

Aimless wandering is especially fruitful in Trinidad – and, since dozens of street names have changed and neither maps nor residents seem sure of what to call many of them, roaming without a plan is the only practical solution. Virtually every street has its own colonial treasure and feast for the eyes.

Valle de los Ingenios viewed from Torre de Manaca-Iznaga

Around Trinidad

Trinidad's prosperity in the 19th century came from the fruits of 50 sugar mills nearby in the scenic **Valle de los Ingenios** (Valley of the Sugar Mills), along with Trinidad a Unesco World Heritage Site. A *mirador* (lookout) with spectacular views is just 5km (3 miles) out of town. About 10km (6 miles) further east is Manaca-Iznaga, where you can explore a lovely colonial hacienda house and its startling, rocket-shaped **Torre de Manaca-Iznaga**. From the top of the tower, the Iznaga family would keep watch over their slaves toiling in the fields. If you don't have a car, you can hire a taxi for about CUC$12 round trip or arrange a trip through Havanatur or Cubatur in Trinidad. A steam train once used in the sugar industry traverses the whole valley for tourists. It leaves from Estación Dragones, the station in the south of Trinidad, at 9.30am and returns at 2–3pm, but make sure you arrive at least 15 minutes before departure.

Those who love beaches will head to **Playa Ancón**, approximately 16km (10 miles) from Trinidad, an excellent strip of white sand and clear waters. Here you'll find diving at an offshore coral reef, a good choice of watersports and three hotels popular with package tourists. Again, you can hire a taxi or pick up a rental bike (give it a test ride as many are pretty primitive; smarter bikes with gears can be hired from next door to the bus station). Another good beach excursion is the daytrip to the tiny island of **Cayo Blanco** from Playa Ancón.

Sierra del Escambray

More compact than the island's eastern and western ranges, the **Sierra del Escambray** (Escambray mountains), coated in luxuriant vegetation, are arguably Cuba's most beautiful range and easily accessible. Blessed with their own micro-climate, the mountains are a wonderfully cool refuge from the heat of Trinidad.

To get to the **Topes de Collantes** national park, take the road west of Trinidad for the steep 15km (9-mile) climb through dense forests of palms, eucalyptus and pines. You'll pass a health resort, a Stalinesque complex that has decent facilities but lacks life. Two excellent hiking trails conclude with beautiful waterfalls: Salto de Caburní, at 62m (203ft), and Salto Vega Grande. Wear sturdy shoes, as each hike is a steep trek of 4km (2½ miles) along a narrow and often muddy trail. You can swim in the chilly

Topes de Collantes

natural pools underneath the falls. Jeep excursions can be hired at any tour agency in Trinidad. There's a CUC$6.50 national park charge.

Sancti Spíritus

Approximately 80km (50 miles) east of Trinidad is **Sancti Spíritus**, one of Diego Velázquez's seven original townships. Although no match for Trinidad, it has some attractive colonial buildings. The **Iglesia Parroquial Mayor de Espíritu Santo** has foundations from 1522, making it the country's oldest (though the present stone church was built in 1680). Nearby is the **Puente Yayabo**, the oldest stone arched bridge in Cuba.

Santa Clara

A must on the itinerary of all fans of the Revolution, Santa Clara is a pleasant university city famous as the last resting place of guerrilla hero, Che Guevara. It was the site of the last battle, which started on 28 December 1958 and finished when news arrived that Batista had fled the country on 1 January 1959. An armoured troop train was heading from Havana to Santiago, but Che and his men ambushed it at Santa Clara. Four of the carriages are preserved at the **Monumento a la Toma del Tren Blindado** (Calle Independencia; Tue–Sat 8am–6pm, Sun 8am–noon; charge). You can go into the carriages and see some of the items carried on the train, as well as photos. At the **Plaza de la Revolución Ernesto Guevara** is a huge statue of Che in battle dress, while underneath is the **mausoleum** (Tue–Sat 8am–9pm, Sun 8am–6pm; free) where Che and his comrades who fell in battle in Bolivia in 1967 were interred when their remains were brought back in 1997. Next to it is the **Museo Histórico de la Revolución** (Tue–Sat 8am–9pm, Sun 8am–5pm), which has displays detailing Che's life and his role in the Revolution.

Cayo Coco and Cayo Guillermo

These two offshore cays are reached by a causeway across the Bahía de Perros so long (28km/17 miles) that you can't see the land at the far end as you set off.

Cayo Coco is named not for coconuts but for a bird: the ibis, as revealed in Hemingway's *Islands in the Stream*. The author patrolled these shores in World War II on the lookout for Nazis. Ibises and other wading birds, often pink flamingoes, can be seen balancing in the brackish waters around the principal causeway and a smaller causeway connecting the cay to **Cayo Guillermo**.

Cayo Guillermo

It's the superb, impossibly white sandy beaches, the intensely blue waters, and the excellent fishing that draw travellers, and there's not much else to distract you. Both cays are covered in forest or thick undergrowth. Large, luxury resorts line the 22km (14 miles) of shell-shaped beaches on Cayo Coco. There are plans to build 1,000 hotel rooms a year until Cayo Coco has 16,000 (it had 5,000 in 2005). A wide range of non-motorised watersports are available to hotel guests; diving and safaris are popular. If you hire a moped or Jeep from your hotel, there are virgin beaches to discover, though with increased development they may no longer be virgin when you get there.

Plaza San Juan de Dios in Camagüey

Camagüey

About 550km (342 miles) southeast of Havana, **Camagüey** is an attractive colonial city; Cuba's third largest. Restrained old façades hide picturesque courtyards, and there are some half-dozen squares, each with an old church. Some, like Nuestra Señora del Carmen and Iglesia San Juan de Dios, have been nicely restored. The province's cattle-grazed plains hold little water, so the citizens fashioned huge earthenware pots to catch rainwater. Called *tinajones*, these still adorn many squares.

The city's most famous son, a general from the Ten Years' War, was born in 1841 at the **Casa Natal de Ignacio Agramonte** (Tue–Sat 10am–5pm, Sun 10am–1pm; charge), a handsome, early 19th-century mansion on Plaza de los Trabajadores in the city centre. The patriot met his death in battle in 1873. **Nuestra Señora de la Merced** church opposite has benefited from recent restoration: the decorated ceiling is particularly striking.

A dashing equine statue of Agramonte forms the centrepiece of **Parque Agramonte**, just to the south. The cathedral occupies one side of the park, and the Casa de la Trova, around a floral patio, has musical performances afternoon and evening.

A 10-minute walk west down Calle Cristo brings you to a dignified 18th-century church, **Santo Cristo del Buen Viaje**. Behind the church is a great sea of crosses and marble saints in a picturesque cemetery. A few blocks north is the triangular-shaped **Plaza del Carmen**, which has been beautifully restored. In one corner stands the **Convento de Nuestra Señora del Carmen**; dating from the early 19th century, the restored church façade is one of the most beautiful in Cuba and is unique in Camagüey for having two towers.

Another splendid feature of Camagüey – and marvellously restored – is **Plaza San Juan de Dios**, an angular old cobble-stoned square surrounded by brightly hued single-storey buildings dating from the 18th century, plus a lovely yellow church with a fine mahogany ceiling and altar, alongside a restored former hospital. It's one of Cuba's most beautiful plazas. A few blocks south, near the river, is an impressive agricultural market. A noisy, lively place, it's open every day and stocked with a surprising array of meat and fresh produce.

Bar on Parque Agramonte

Playa Santa Lucía

An hour-and-a-half drive (110km/68 miles) from Camagüey on the north coast, remote **Playa Santa Lucía** beckons sun worshippers with resort hotels strung along a particularly fine peninsular strip of sand. Each hotel backs directly onto the beach. A superb coral reef lies offshore, and diving here is excellent. Aside from a couple of roadside bars, however, nightlife is limited to hotel entertainment. The only other drawback is the mosquitoes, as voracious as anywhere on the island, though the hotels do spray daily – good for visitors, but bad for the environment.

To counter the isolation of Playa Santa Lucía, the tourist authorities offer a wide range of excursions, including a rodeo at Rancho King, deep-sea fishing, and boat and helicopter trips for days on the beach at such unspoiled cays as Cayo Sabinal and Cayo Saetía. A bus service visits **Playa Los Cocos**, some 5km (3 miles) away; with sheltered aquamarine waters, it's a strong contender for the title of 'Cuba's most beautiful beach'. Adjacent is La Boca, a very small community of waterside shacks with fish restaurants.

ORIENTE: THE EAST

Prior to the Revolution, the east of Cuba was a single province known simply as **Oriente** ('East'), and most Cubans still refer to the region with this name. Oriente incorporates the post-revolutionary provinces of Holguín, Granma, Santiago de Cuba and Guantánamo, which are scenically and historically more interesting than most of central Cuba. The stunning landscapes vary from the north coast's exuberant banana and coconut groves clustered round thatched huts, little changed

Fidel Castro with brother Raúl, Sierra Maestra, 1957

Beach life beneath the Sierra Maestra

from earlier indigenous peoples' *bohíos*, to the towering peaks of the Sierra Maestra mountains and lush rainforest on the east coast. Some of Cuba's best beaches lie on the north coast of Oriente within sight of the mountains.

The wars of independence began in Oriente in the 1860s, and nearly a century later Castro concentrated his power base in the inaccessible Sierra Maestra. There are stirring monuments and museums recalling these periods in Santiago de Cuba, the latter dubbed a 'heroic city' for its many historic patriots.

The further east you travel in Cuba the more Caribbean it feels. Santiago de Cuba is renowned for its contributions to Cuban musical culture; the Oriente is the heartland of *son*, the traditional rural music that formed the roots of salsa, and many of the genre's greats (Trío Matamoros, La Vieja Trova Santiaguera and Elíades Ochoa, among others) got their start in Santiago.

Holguín Province

Playa Esmeralda

The province of Holguín begins bleakly around the busy capital but improves considerably as you travel north, where the countryside is lusher. **Guardalavaca**, 60km (37 miles) from Holguín, is perhaps Cuba's most attractive resort, ringed by banana plantations and facing a gorgeous beach backed by a forest of sea-grape trees. Watersports are excellent here and at the equally picturesque – but isolated – **Playa Esmeralda**, 2km (1 mile) west. All-inclusive hotels are dotted along the coast to the west, occupying horseshoe bays and sandy beaches such as Playa Pesquero Viejo and Playa Pesquero Nuevo.

There are plenty of possibilities for excursions in the vicinity of Guardalavaca. To the west is **Bahía de Bariay**, which has a monument claiming Columbus's landing (a fact contested chiefly by Baracoa, further east). Beyond the bay is **Gibara** (27km/17 miles north of Holguín), a captivating if sleepy little port town. You can take a boat trip into the middle of Bahía de Naranjo to a simple aquarium, or arrange sailing and fishing trips from the marina.

About 6km (4 miles) south of Guardalavaca, on a hill amid a forest of palms and thatched homesteads, is **Chorro de Maíta** (Tue–Sat 9am–5pm, Sun 9am–1pm; charge), the Caribbean's most important excavated Indian burial ground. Fifty-six of the 180 skeletons found are on display. They date from 1490 to 1540 and lie exactly as they were found. All but one are Amerindian, buried in the Central American style with arms folded across stomachs. The one Spaniard lies in a Christian fashion with arms crossed on his chest.

Banana groves coat the hillsides along the scenic 30km (19-mile) route south to **Banes**, a town of wooden houses with corrugated roofs. Castro was married at the church here in 1948, and the town's **Museo Indo-Cubano** has some fascinating finds from Chorro de Maíta.

Santiago de Cuba

Many visitors prefer Cuba's second city (population 554,000) to the capital. **Santiago de Cuba** (880km/546 miles south-east of Havana) is one of the oldest cities, with a wealth of colonial buildings. Unfailingly vibrant and seductive, it exudes a feel all its own. Enclosed by the Sierra Maestra mountains, Santiago can also be wickedly hot. *Santiagueros* negotiate their hilly streets by keeping to the shady sides, and they relax on overhanging balconies.

Making music in Santiago

Santiago is Cuba's melting pot, with a friendly population of predominantly mulatto people: descendants of Spanish, French from Haiti, Jamaicans and huge numbers of African slaves. Afro-Cuban traditions remain strong, reflected in in *carnaval,* which is still Cuba's best, and in music (walk down any street and a cacophony of sounds will emanate from unseen sources).

Founded in 1514, Santiago was the island's capital until 1553. It is regarded as a 'heroic city' *(ciudad héroe)*, and locals are proud of the city's rebellious past. Seminal events brought it centre-stage again during the 1950s, when it assumed a major role in the revolutionary struggle. The attack on Batista's forces at the Moncada Barracks in 1953 thrust Fidel Castro into the national limelight, and it was in Santiago's main square that he first declared victory, on 1 January 1959.

Old Santiago

The most atmospheric part of the city is **Old Santiago**. Castro delivered his victory speech in the heart of the old town, from the balcony of city hall on **Parque Céspedes**. More a plaza than a park, the attractive square is a genteel place with tall trees, gas lanterns and iron benches. Old Santiago's grid of streets unfolds here, a few blocks inland from the heavily industrialised harbour. Parque Céspedes is dominated by its twin-towered **cathedral**. A basilica was built on this spot in 1528, but what you see was rebuilt in the early 19th century after a series of earthquakes and fires.

On the west side of the plaza is **Casa de Diego Velázquez** (daily 9am–4.30pm; charge). Noticeable for its black-slatted balconies, it was built in 1516 as the residence of the founder of Cuba's original seven *villas*. The oldest house in Cuba and one of the oldest in the Americas, it is in remarkable condition. Housing the **Museo de Ambiente Histórico Cubano**, its rooms overflow with period furniture and carved woodwork and encircle two lovely courtyards. Disregard the poor reproductions of original wall murals around the courtyard.

Across the square is the elegant **Hotel Casa Granda**, which opened in 1914. Its terrace bar on the fifth floor affords excellent views of the cathedral towers and the city beyond.

East from the square, **Calle Heredia** is the epicentre of Santiago culture and tourism. The city's famous **Casa de la Trova** (music hall), which has hosted nearly all legendary Cuban musicians, is the centrepiece of both. Starting in mid-morning, a succession of groups perform every style of Cuban music here, from *son* and *guarachas* to *boleros* and *salsa*. The intimate open-air space inside is the place to be in the evenings; at night the main groups play upstairs. Calle Heredia is lined by day with artisans and souvenir sellers.

Down the street is the **Museo del Carnaval**, a museum containing instruments, photos and artefacts from Santiago's carnival. It also has Afro-Cuban music and dance (Sun–Fri at 4pm), as does the **Artex** store up the street. Also on Calle Heredia is the **Casa Natal de José María Heredia** (Tue–Sat 9am–8pm; charge), the birthplace of the early 19th-century Cuban poet and a cultural centre and museum.

The cathedral on Parque Céspedes

Nearby, on Calle Pío Rosado, the **Museo Provincial Emilio Bacardí** (Mon noon–8pm, Tue–Sat 10am–8pm, Sun 9am–1pm; charge) has a first-rate collection of Cuban art, as well as some European works, some items from the wars of independence and an archaeological hall that features a 3,000-year-old Egyptian mummy, two Peruvian skeletons and a shrunken head. The museum, in a grandiose neo-classical building on a beguiling little street, is named for its benefactor and the town's former mayor, whose family founded the Bacardí rum empire.

One of Santiago's most delightful people-watching spots is **Plaza Dolores**, a shady plaza lined with colonial-era homes (several now house tourist restaurants).

Museo Provincial Emilio Bacardí

Avenida José A. Saco (more commonly known as **Enramada**) is Santiago's main shopping thorough-fare. Its faded 1950s neon signs and ostentatious build-ings recall more prosperous times. Cobbled **Calle Bar-tolomé Masó** (also known as San Basilio), just behind Heredia and the cathedral, is a delightful street that leads down to the picturesque Tivolí district.

In Tivolí you'll find the famous **Padre Pico** steps, named for a Santiaguero priest who aided the city's poor. Castro once roared fire and brimstone down on the

Batista government here, but today you'll find more pacific chess and domino players who have set up all-hours tables on the steps. Take the steps up to the **Museo de la Lucha Clandestina**, the Museum of the Clandestine Struggle (Tue–Sun 9am– 5pm; charge). This excellent museum, in one of the city's finest colonial houses, foc-

Bacardí's bat

Bacardí moved its head- quarters and production to Puerto Rico after the Revolution, and from there to Bermuda. But it was the fruit bats that nested in the rafters of the original rum factory in Santiago that gave Bacardi rum its world- famous bat logo.

uses on the activities of the resistance movement under local martyr Frank País. Residents of Santiago were instrumental in supporting the Revolution, as were peasants in the Sierra Maestra. From the museum's balcony, there are tremendous views of Santiago and the bay (and, unfortunately, of plumes of pollution rising up from ill-placed factories).

Not far from the museum is one of Santiago's best places to get sweaty in the evening. The **Casa de las Tradiciones**, a 'cultural centre' in a sweet little pink house (Calle General Lacret, 651), has live music and as much dancing as its tiny space will allow. Known locally as La Casona, it's great fun, and local people usually outnumber tourists. Couples only.

Just west of the Padre Pico steps (south of the railway station) is the one-room **César Escalante cigar factory**, unimpressive by comparison with other Cuban cigar factories but enjoyable to visit; and the **Ron Caney** rum distillery, the oldest in Cuba, established in 1838 by Don Facundo Bacardí (whose descendants fled the country in 1959) and nationalised in 1960. The rum produced here now goes under the names of 'Caney' and 'Santiago de Cuba'. You can visit only a shop and bar.

Around Santiago

A good place to get your bearings on the suburbs of the city is from the rooftop bar of the lavish hotel Meliá Santiago, 3km (almost 2 miles) east of the city's centre. In the near distance you can make out the yellow **Moncada Barracks**, which Castro, along with around 100 rebels attacked on 26 July 1953. The date is now a rallying cry and public holiday, and the barracks have been converted into a school and museum, known both as the **Antiguo Cuartel Moncada** and the **Museo Histórico 26 de Julio** (Av. Moncada esq. Gen. Portuondo; Tue–Sat 9am–7.30pm, Sun 9am–1pm; charge; guided tour available in Spanish, English, French or Italian). The museum tells the story of the road to revolution using dozens of memorable photographs. Also on display are various bloodstained rebel uniforms, some of Fidel's personal effects from his time in the mountains, and '26 Julio' armbands (sporting the name of the resistance movement that developed after the Moncada attack). The bullet holes over the entrance were 'restored' from photos.

North of Moncada, by the bus station, is the **Plaza de la Revolución**, an open square at the corner of Av. las Américas and Av. de los Libertadores. Massive machetes (used by *mambí* independence fighters) thrust towards the sky in this monument to Antonio Maceo, a hero of the war of independence, who is seen riding triumphantly.

The fine **Cementerio Santa Ifigenia**, just north of the harbour (Av. Crombet, Reparto Juan Gómez), is the resting place of many Cuban heroes. Pride of place goes to the Cuban founding father José Martí, in a vast octagonal mausoleum designed so that the tomb catches the sun throughout the day. An armed guard is changed ceremoniously every half hour. Céspedes is buried here too, as are the remains of 38 of the martyrs of the 26 July movement. They are interred in a wall just inside the entrance; each 'brick' is marked with a name.

In an impressive setting 7km (4 miles) from the city is the 17th-century **Castillo del Morro** (daily 8am–8pm; charge), surveying the harbour mouth from a commanding clifftop position. Moated, thick-walled, and full of cannons, drawbridges and passageways, it is in fine condition. One room houses displays on pirates through the ages. A guide will point out a torture room with a trap door in the floor, through which uncooperative prisoners and slaves were reportedly dropped into the sea below. The restaurant near the fortress, also called 'El Morro', has

Castillo del Morro

gorgeous views of the sea and some of Santiago's finest food; it's a great place to get out of the intense sun. The easiest way to get to El Morro is to hire a taxi, which costs between CUC$10 and 15 for the round trip (the driver will wait while you explore the fortress and even eat lunch).

A place of great import (and considerable beauty) is the triple-domed **Basílica del Cobre** (daily 6.30am–6pm) named after the nearby copper mines that rise out of the forested foothills 18km (11 miles) west of Santiago. Cuban faithful make annual pilgrimages to the church to pay tribute to its statue of a black virgin, the Virgen de la Caridad (Virgin of Charity), Cuba's patron saint. According to legend, in 1606 three young fishermen struggling in their storm-tossed boat out in the bay were saved by the miraculous appearance of the Virgin, who was holding a mulatto baby Jesus in one hand and a cross in the other. Pilgrims, often making the last of the trek on their knees, pray to her image and place mementos and offerings of thanks for her miracles; among them are small boats and prayers for those who have tried to escape Cuba on rafts. Except during Mass, the Virgin is kept on the second floor, encased in glass and cloaked in a glittering gold robe.

You can take a taxi to El Cobre for around CUC$20 roundtrip, although the more adventurous can catch a *colectivo* (bus or truck) out to the town and walk the couple of kilometres to the church. If you'd like to stay overnight in this spectacular (and peaceful) area, there is a *hostal*, **Hospedería de la Caridad**, behind the church.

Basílica del Cobre

East of Santiago is **Parque Baconao**, a biosphere reserve spread over 40km (25 miles). The local dark-sand beaches can be scrubby and the hotels themselves are isolated, but there's lots to explore in the park, and the Sierra de La Gran Piedra rise majestically above the coast. A tortuous side road 12km (7 miles) east along the coast ascends the mountains to **La Gran Piedra** (Great Stone), where you can climb on foot for a bird's-eye view of eastern Cuba. About 2km (1 mile) beyond, a track leads to the

Cafetal-Museo La Isabelica, a 19th-century coffee-plantation *finca* (country house) with a workshop, original furniture and a terrace where coffee beans were once laid out to dry. The museum (Tue–Sat 9am–4pm, Sun 9am–1pm; charge) is part of the Unesco World Heritage Site that protects the architectural legacy of early 19th-century coffee farms.

GUANTÁNAMO PROVINCE

You can reach Cuba's remote, mountainous, far-eastern region from Santiago. The province has only one true tourist draw, but it's a super one: the magical little town of Baracoa. The only reason to stop near the unappealing city of Guantánamo would be to visit the lookout point trained on the US naval base with its controversial Camp Delta detention centre, built in 2002 to hold foreign terror suspects captured during the war against the Taliban and Al Qaeda in Afghanistan. To visit the Mirador de Malones lookout, you must arrange your trip in advance through one of the central tour agencies in Santiago; vouchers cost about CUC$5 per person. The lookout can be visited en route to Baracoa; there is no need to overnight in Guantánamo.

'Gitmo'

Guantánamo, known to American military personnel as 'Gitmo', is a curious anomaly in revolutionary Cuba. Where in the world is the US less likely to have a military base? Established in 1903 – making it the oldest overseas American naval base – the lease was effectively forced on the Cubans by an interventionist US administration. The US still sends its annual rent cheques (about US$4,000), which haven't been cashed since 1960. To do so would be to recognise the legitimacy of the American presence in Cuba.

Baracoa

The dry, cactus-strewn landscape of the south coast begins to change as you follow the winding, spectacular 30km (18-mile) road 'La Farola' across the mountains to **Baracoa** (150km/93 miles from Santiago), a picturesque little village known for its local chocolate and coconut factories. The tropical seaside town is surrounded by green hillsides covered with cocoa and coconut groves, and all around are palm-backed beaches. Baracoa lies smack in the middle of the wettest region in Cuba, and has no fewer than 10 rivers, all of them ripe for whitewater rafting. In the mountains to the northwest is the Parque Nacional Alejandro de Humboldt, a biosphere reserve named after the great German naturalist and explorer.

Baracoa was the first settlement to be established by Diego Velázquez in 1511. Columbus came here first, though, after landing at Bariay Bay in today's Holguín province in October 1492, and planted the Cruz de la Parra (Cross of the Vine) in the soil on his arrival. What is claimed to be this cross is on display in **Nuestra Señora de la Asunción**, the church on Plaza Independencia.

Baracoa has so much going for it that any associations with Columbus are a bonus. A good place to get your bearings is the hilltop **Hotel El Castillo**, a former castle looking out over red-tiled roofs, the town's expansive, oyster-shaped bay and the landmark mountain called El Yunque (The Anvil), named for its singular shape.

In the main square is a striking bust of Hatuey, the brave Indian leader who resisted early *conquistadores* until he was caught by the Spanish and burned at the stake. There's also a charming and very lively Casa de la Trova here. It is worth wandering along the Malecón, the seaside avenue, from the snug **Fuerte Matachín** (an early 19th-century fort that has a small but informative municipal museum inside and a hulking statue of Columbus outside) to the Hotel La Rusa, which is named after a legendary and glamorous Russian émigrée who over the years hosted celebrities such as Che Guevara, Fidel Castro and Errol Flynn.

In and around Baracoa are several dozen pre-Columbian archaeological sites related to the two major indigenous groups that once inhabited the region. There is an endearing little **Museo Arqueológico** (officially 9am–6pm, but hours vary; charge) in **Las Cuevas del Paraíso** up the hill from the village, which contains a copy of the Taíno tobacco idol found nearby in 1903 (the original is in Havana).

Baracoa: first Spanish settlement on Cuba, and famous for its rain

WHAT TO DO

ENTERTAINMENT

Although cultural activity has been under state control since the revolution and Havana no longer sizzles with the sleazy Mafia-funded casinos and clubs of the 1950s, both high culture and down-to-earth nightlife thrive in Cuba. Outside the resorts, it can be hard to pin down what's going on where, but informal musical performances are ubiquitous. In the resorts, nightlife is focused around hotels, ranging from decent live bands, dance and fashion shows to Beatles sing-alongs.

Live Music Performances

Cubans crave live music, and – with the surge in international popularity of traditional Cuban music – so do most visitors to Cuba. You certainly won't have to go out of your way to hear music performances. Roving groups of musicians can be found playing everywhere from airports to restaurants. Merely wandering the streets of Havana, Santiago or Trinidad, you're likely to stumble across a party with a live band, or even a back alley where some impromptu jamming is going on. On Saturday nights in Camagüey, the music spreads to the streets in a 'Noche Camagüeya' block party along Calle República.

All the styles of Cuba's traditional music – *habaneras, son, boleros, guarachas, guajiras* and more – can be heard in every town's *casa de la trova*, usually a fine old building on or near the main square. Performances take place afternoons and evenings. Especially in the evenings and on weekends, when you'll encounter a vibrant mix of Cubans and foreigners, the island's *casas de la trova* really swing. The most famous is in

Cabaret in full swing at the Tropicana

A sedate alternative to salsa

Santiago de Cuba, while those in towns like Trinidad, Baracoa, Camagüey and Holguín are great fun.

Aside from traditional acoustic music, Cuba revels in salsa. In Havana the salsa dance fan can choose from a number of venues every night and some matinées as well. They feature top salsa groups, but cover charges are still quite low. Because the clubs cater to foreigners, the level of dance skill is mixed; generally the more Cubans there are in the audience the better. Music hotspots include:

Havana. Casa de la Música Miramar (salsa; Avenida 35 and Calle 20, Miramar), Casa de la Música (salsa; Calle Galiano e/ Concordia y Neptuno, Central Havana), Casa de la Trova (traditional music; San Lázaro, 661 e/ Gervasio y Belascoaín, Central Havana), Copa Room (formerly the Palacio de la Salsa) in the Hotel Riviera (salsa; Paseo y Malecón, in Vedado) and la Zorra y el Cuervo (jazz; Calles 23 y O, Vedado).

Trinidad. Casa de la Trova (traditional music; Fernando Echerri 29, e/ Jesús Menéndez y Patricio Lumumba), Casa de la Música (salsa and various live acts; two venues on the Escalinata near the Plaza Mayor), Palenque de los Congos Reales (Afro-Cuban folkloric show; Fernando Echerri half a block away towards the Plaza Mayor).

Santiago de Cuba. Casa de la Trova (Calle Heredia), Casa de las Tradiciones (Calle General Lacret).

Baracoa. Casa de la Trova (José Martí, 149) and Casa de la Cultura (Maceo, 124).

Cabaret

A legacy of the high-rolling casino days in Cuba, cabarets have been kept alive and well as an outlet for tourist dollars. Cavorting mulatta dancers in sparkling G-strings and pairs of strategically placed stars may not be most peoples' image of socialist doctrine – but this is Caribbean communism. While the best shows (at the Tropicana clubs in both Havana and Santiago de Cuba) are rather expensive by Cuban

A Musical Melting Pot

Salsa, rumba, mambo, *cha-cha-chá*, *son*, *danzón* – Cuba's rhythms are known the world over. Reflecting the mixed heritage of its people, Cuban music spontaneously combusted towards the end of the 1800s through the nexus of African and European cultures – in particular what's been described as the love affair between the African drum and the Spanish guitar. In a typical Cuban band today you'll hear Latin stringed instruments in harmony with congas, *timbales* and African bongos (all drums), *claves* (wooden sticks) and instruments made from hollow gourds such as the maracas and the *güiro*. Cuban percussionists are among the finest in the world.

First came *son* ('sound'), a style that originated in Oriente around the turn of the 20th century. Son permeates all Cuban music and is the direct forebear of salsa; it has a percussive swing that is intrinsically Cuban. Mixed with jazz influences, it led to the brass-band salsa of famous groups such as Los Van Van, Isaac Delgado and Irakere. *Cha-cha-chá* arrived in the 1950s, having developed from mambo, itself a blend of jazz and the sedate, European *danzón* of the ballroom. The strongly Afro-Cuban rumba is typified by heavy drumming and more celebratory, erotic dancing. *Trovas* (ballads) were sung in colonial times by troubadors in *casas de la trova*. After the revolution the *trova* evolved into the *nueva trova*, often with overtly political lyrics, made popular by such artists as Silvio Rodríguez and Pablo Milanés.

standards, seeing at least one big song-and-dance production in the flesh (so to speak) is de rigueur.

The Tropicana in Havana (Calle 72 #4504 e/ 43 y 45, Marianao, tel: 07-267 0110), founded in 1939, is indisputably the queen of cabarets. The likes of Nat King Cole performed here in pre-revolutionary times. With a 32-piece orchestra and a cast of over 200 (some parading in impossibly large headdresses), in a dazzling open-air arena, the sheer scale of the spectacle will make your head spin. Tickets cost from CUC$70–90, including a quarter bottle of rum and a mixer. Book at your hotel reception or buy tickets at the entrance between 8.30 and 9pm. The show starts at 10pm and lasts 1 hour 45 minutes, after which you can head to the club. Havana's next-best cabaret show, smaller and half the price, is Cabaret Parisien, at the Hotel Nacional (Calles 21 and O, Vedado, tel: 07-333 564; nightly at 10pm).

The Tropicana in Santiago de Cuba (Autopista Nacional km 1.5, Wed–Sun only; tel: 0122-687 020, 642 579) fills an enormous, recently constructed complex on the city's northern outskirts. It is no less impressive than Havana's but tickets are less expensive (CUC$50 with one drink included); get there for 9.30pm in time for the main show at 10pm.

In Varadero, the Cabaret Continental at the Hotel Internacional (Ave Las Américas; tel: 0145-667 038; Tue–Sat, 8pm for dinner, 10pm for the show; CUC$40 with dinner, CUC$25 without) pales in comparison with the former venues but is nonetheless an enjoyable and sometimes fairly raunchy song-and-dance extravaganza.

A fun show – kind of Afro-Cuban with a pirate theme – followed by a disco, takes place in a cave at the Cueva del Pirata, some 9km (6 miles) east of Varadero (Autopista Sur, km 11), Mon–Sat at 10pm until the wee hours. There is also a cabaret at the Meliá Varadero hotel.

In Trinidad, you can hear traditional music at the Casa de la Trova (Fernando Echerri 29, e/ Jesús Menéndez y Patricio Lumumba; 9am–1am, with a show starting at 9pm; admission charge at night). Also in Trinidad, there's an Afro-Cuban folkloric show at the open-air Palenque de los Congos Reales (9pm–2am, with the show starting at 10pm; admission charge) half a block away towards the Plaza Mayor. Or head to the Casa de la Música, at the top of the Escalinata near the Plaza Mayor, to see various live acts.

Discos

Discos pulsate to both Latin and Euro-American rhythms. The places to be are Habana Café (the disco in Havana's Hotel Meliá Cohiba) and the disco in Santiago's eponymous hotel. These are glitzy affairs, where foreigners get merry and approached by hustlers of all stripes. Varadero has Palacio

Sabado dance at El Palenque in Havana

de La Rumba at the end of Avenue Las Américas, which is popular with a young crowd and has live salsa bands at weekends; or Mambo Club – on the Autopista Sur, further down the peninsula, by the Gran Hotel – which is similar but with live music. Entrance is CUC$10 in both cases, but you get free national drinks at the bar. In Trinidad, the Discoteca Las Cuevas really gets going at 1am, when the other music venues in town close. In Guardalavaca, head for open-air La Roca, set just above the beach.

Bars and Cafés

Both bars and cafés are places to have a mojito, daiquiri or shot of *ron* (rum), smoke a Cohiba, and – usually – hear some live Cuban rhythms. In Havana the bars not to miss are Hemingway haunts: La Bodeguita del Medio and El Floridita. Enjoyable café-bars in Havana include Café de

Havana's El Floridita: a legendary haunt

Paris (Obispo y San Ignacio), Café O'Reilly (O'Reilly y San Ignacio), Monserrate (Monserrate y Obrapía) and El Patio (Plaza de la Catedral). There are also several places on Plaza Vieja, including Cervecería Taberna de La Muralla with home-brewed malt beer; and on the opposite corner, the Café Taberna at Mercaderes esq. Teniente Rey, done up in 1950s style and dedicated to the late, great Cuban singer, Beny Moré. Several hotels also have good bars, including Hotel Sevilla (made famous in Graham Greene's *Our Man in Havana*), Hotel Inglaterra's rooftop bar and Hotel Havana Libre's Turquino (with amazing views from the 25th floor).

In Santiago de Cuba, the terrace bar on the fifth floor of the Hotel Casa Granda has fine views and live music. A good place for a cold beer is Taberna Dolores, which often has live music in its courtyard. At the corner of Calle Calvario is Café Isabelica, a venerable 24-hour bohemian haunt in a house three centuries old. It's the kind of place where tourists and Cubans seem to hook up in a matter of seconds. Baracoa's Hotel Castillo has a bar with sensational views and frequent live music.

Classical Repertoire

The classical arts are greatly valued in Cuba, and drama, opera, classical music recitals and above all ballet can be enjoyed in theatres all around Cuba. Opulent, old-fashioned theatres such as those in Cienfuegos, Camagüey and Matanzas, not to mention Havana's magnificent Gran Teatro, are sights in their own right. The best way to learn what's on is to visit the theatre; performances are frequently limited to weekends.

The Gran Teatro in Havana, at Prado y San José (tel: 07-861 3077), has two main concert halls and puts on a wide repertoire of entertainment, from opera recitals to ballet. It is home to the internationally renowned Ballet Nacional de Cuba; if you hear that the company (or the rather more innovative Ballet de Camagüey) is performing, be sure to snap up tickets.

Havana's International Ballet Festival is held during the last week of October and first week of November.

Visitors to Santiago de Cuba should try to see the Ballet Folklórico Cutumba, a renowned troupe that delves into the world of Afro-Cuban spirituality and ritual. They perform at several theatres when in town.

SHOPPING

Shopping in Havana

Cuba has a reputation as a destination where there's little worth buying. You will see incredibly barren shops – window displays with bottles of cooking oil, shoe polish and a few plumbing parts. But there are plenty of things for visitors to buy. The dual currency system means that you pay for your goods in *pesos convertibles* (CUCs), while Cubans pay for their basic goods in *pesos Cubanos*, or *moneda nacional* (CUPs). Top on most people's lists are Cuba's greatest achievements (not including its health care system): cigars, rum and music. There is also an excellent selection of handicrafts, and tourist markets are now thriving in Cuba's major centres, even if much of what you'll find is related to Che Guevara – berets, T-shirts bearing his countenance, and dolls, among many other 'revolutionary' items.

As for essentials, hotel and dollar shops (as the CUC shops are still called) carry mineral water, soap, shampoo, toilet paper and toothpaste, and these items are now sometimes available from small kiosk shops. However, it's still best to bring all your medicinal or cosmetic staples from home. Tiendas Panamericanas are well-stocked stores, but probably the most impressive store in all Cuba is the Harris Bros. Company, a multistorey enterprise near the landmark Art Deco Bacardí building and the Capitolio.

Cuban cities are now an uneasy mix of sad *peso Cubano* stores and bright *peso convertible* shops with goods most Cubans can only dream about (indeed, you'll see large crowds of people peering dreamily into shop windows). The uneven divide between communist ideals and materialist longings is one of the great contradictions in contemporary Cuba. Browsing along shopping streets proves endlessly fascinating though, and provides insights into Cuba's arcane economy.

Souvenirs to Buy

Cigars and rum. The biggest bargain in Cuba is probably a coveted box of premium cigars, which at home might cost four times more. Cigar factories have affiliated shops selling all brands of cigars; the Partagás factory in Havana has a particularly good shop, as does the specialist cigar hotel in Old Havana: Hostal Conde de Villanueva at Mercaderes 202. You can also purchase cigars at shops such as Casa del Tabaco (Calle Obispo and Bernaza) and La Casa del Habano (Calle Mercaderes, 120) in Havana, at hotels and at the airport. You will find Habanos shops in

Export permits

If you purchase anything that can be described as art – even a cheap watercolour at a flea market – you'll need an official export permit to get it out of the country without hassle or fear of confiscation. Most official galleries should be able to provide you with this – a purchase receipt will not usually be sufficient.

El Puro: The Cuban Cigar

Before launching the US trade embargo against Cuba, President Kennedy reportedly had an aide round up a supply of his favourite Cuban cigars. Now that cigars have again become chic, almost everyone knows that Cuban *puros* are reputed to be the world's finest. Factories produce more than 350 million cigars a year, with 100 million for export. Before the revolution there were more than 1,000 Cuban brands of cigars; today there are only about three dozen.

You can visit a number of cigar factories, where the rich aroma is overwhelming. *Torcedores* (the men and women who roll the cigars) wrap the different types of leaves (some for taste, burn, etc) inside the wrapper leaves with dexterous ease. Sacks of tobacco leaves are sorted into bundles, cigars undergo quality control tests, and prestigious labels are applied. Handmade cigars vary in length from the 4.5-inch Demi Tasse to the 9.25-inch Gran Corona. As a rule, bigger cigars are of better quality and darker-coloured cigars taste sweeter. Back home, keep your cigars moist: place them in a humidor or put the box in a plastic bag with a damp sponge.

Buying a box of cigars can be daunting. People on the street will whisper 'You want cigar, my friend?' and tell you that their sister (or mother or cousin) works in the factory and that the cigars are stolen. They may be hot, but they may also be inferior-quality fakes. Don't buy unless you know what you're doing. Proper-looking boxes are no assurance of authenticity, though official cigars have a new holographic seal on the box. In a shop, ask to look inside the box, take out a cigar, see if you like the aroma, and check for uniform colour. The cigars should be slightly springy.

Fakes are liable to confiscation by customs. In official shops, make sure you keep the two copies of the official receipt – one of these is for you and one is to be given to customs when leaving the country. Keep cigars in your hand luggage for inspection. You are allowed to take up to 23 individual cigars out of the country without a receipt.

several other towns (Trinidad's is on Lino Pérez, 296).

Bottles of Cuban rum also offer big savings. All tourist shops sell rum, whether aged from three to seven years (*añejo*) or low-grade *aguardiente* (from sugarcane alcohol) with humorous labels. Havana Club is the brand of choice and aficionados should visit the distillery's **Museo del Ron** (Av. del Puerto, 262 e/ Sol y Muralla) for a tour and rum tasting, as well as the shop attached.

Quality control

Above El Floridita, Havana's Casa del Ron has the most impressive selection of rums, including hundred-dollar vintages, half a dozen national brands, and rum flavoured with grenadine, peppermint or banana. The airport's duty-free shop also has a wide selection. When buying cigars or rum, bear in mind the customs limits in your home country *(see page 111)*.

Music recordings. CDs and cassettes of Cuban music are widely available. If you're in the market for Cuban recordings, look for the EGREM label, available in Artex stores (as well as others). Most are CUC$15 each. Recommended recordings include those by Trio Matamoros, Beny Moré, Celina González, La Vieja Trova Santiaguero, Los Compadres, Los Zafiros, El Cuarteto Patria, Los Van Van and Pablo Milanés, to name just a few of Cuba's most popular musicians. Musical instruments such as maracas, *claves* and bongos also make good presents.

Handicrafts. Local arts and crafts vary from tacky figurines to pleasant drawings of street scenes and postmodernist portraits. You'll also find evocative posters and black-and-white photos of Fidel, Che and company. Fine handmade lace and crochet are available, principally in Trinidad. You might want to pick up a *guayabera*, the classic Cuban pleated, four-pocketed shirt, worn untucked. Boutique Quitrín (Obispo esq. San Ignacio in Old Havana) has the nicest cotton versions of the original white *guayabera*. Much of the silver-plated jewellery is also a good buy, but you should not purchase anything with black coral – it's endangered and illegal to import in many countries.

There are more interesting things to buy in Old Havana than in the rest of Cuba put together. A lively open-air crafts market (Wed–Sat) is held east of the cathedral plaza between Tacón and the bay. Plaza de Armas is busy with second-hand booksellers (Wed–Sat). Arts and crafts shops are concentrated along Calle Obispo. The excellent Palacio de la Artesanía (at Calle Cuba, 64 e/ Peña Pobre y Cuarteles) is a souvenir supermarket.

Outside Havana, Trinidad has the best array of crafts shops in the country. Several streets just south of the Plaza Mayor (around the *Casa de la Trova*), known as La Candonga, stage a vibrant daily crafts market, and you'll find good government-run crafts shops on Simón Bolívar. Santiago de Cuba's crafts mecca is among the shops and vendors along Calle Heredia. The selection, though, is generally poorer than in Havana.

SPORTS

Watersports

Watersports enthusiasts are in luck in Cuba. Virtually every resort offers windsurfing, sailing, scuba diving and snorkelling. As anywhere in the world, motorised sports are expensive. Watersports centres are almost always affiliated with a particular hotel, but anyone may rent the equipment.

Divers at the Bay of Pigs

Diving is the area of greatest interest and growth. Cuba claims to be surrounded by one of the world's largest coral reefs, and over 1,000 sunken wrecks. There are so many tropical fish and sponges that it can feel like swimming in an aquarium. Facilities are generally excellent, and prices are the lowest in the Caribbean. Nearly every resort has at least one professional diving centre equipped with all the requisite equipment, from oxygen tanks to wetsuits. Most centres offer week-long diving courses for an internationally recognised qualification, as well as two-day introductory courses.

Dozens of dive sites can be reached from resorts, typically a half-hour boat journey away. The diving centre at El Colony Hotel on the Isla de la Juventud offers the best facilities and diving, but it isn't well suited to beginners. Resorts catering to all levels of ability include Playa Santa Lucía, María la Gorda, Cayo Largo, Varadero, Playa Girón (with good diving directly off the shore), Playa Ancón, Cayo Coco and Guardalavaca.

Young baseball player

Deep-sea fishing is one of Cuba's great attractions, as of yet not well known (or over-fished). Trips leave from the island's resorts and Havana's Hemingway Marina in search of marlin, wahoo, swordfish and tarpon. Playas del Este, Varadero and Cayo Largo are other places that offer excellent fishing expeditions. In addition, there are offshore expeditions for smaller fry such as sea bass and mackerel. For freshwater fishing, Hanabanilla and Zaza (near Sancti Spíritus) lakes both hold impressively big, copious large-mouth bass.

Spectator Sports

The national sport is baseball (béisbol). Cuban teams are among the best in the world (several stars have defected to the US major leagues). While children improvise with a stick and a makeshift ball in every town's open spaces, the main cities have vast stadiums. It can be difficult to find out exactly when a game is taking place; you should simply ask around.

CUBA FOR CHILDREN

At resorts, water-loving babies will be happy; those ages 10 and up will be able to join in many of the activities. A few resort hotels (such as those at Cayo Coco) have children's clubs, and top hotels can arrange babysitting. Outside the resorts facilities are limited, transport can be problematic, and feeding fussy children may present difficulties. But Cubans adore children and will certainly make a fuss over yours. Travelling with young families in Cuba can be a remarkable – and eye-opening – experience. If you travel with very young children, be sure to take all the diapers and baby food you require, as these items are hard to find in Cuba. If travelling by hire car, you should supply your own car seat.

Calendar of Events

The Buró de Convenciones (Hotel Neptuno, Calle 3 e/70 y 74, Miramar; tel: 7-204 8273) has information and contact details for all of the festivals and conferences held throughout the year all over the country.

January New Year (1 January, public holiday). Celebrated throughout the country and taking in Liberation Day marking the end of the Batista dictatorship, with music, dancing and outdoor parties.

May May Day (1 May, public holiday) is a big event with parades and speeches in all the Plazas de la Revolución in every town.

June Hemingway Marlin Fishing Tournament (Hemingway Marina, Havana). Four-day competition begun in 1950 and won by Castro in 1960.

18–27 July *Carnaval* (Santiago de Cuba). Cuba's most famous celebration, featuring *comparsas* (street dances), takes in Santiago's patron saint's day on the 25th, but stops temporarily on the 26th in memory of the attack on the Moncada barracks in 1953.

October–November Havana International Ballet Festival. A gathering of top ballet companies from around the world, begun in 1960 and held in alternate years.

December New Latin American Film Festival (Havana). The most important film festival in the Spanish-speaking world, held during the first two weeks of the month. International Jazz Festival (Havana). A biennial, week-long festival, which attracts top jazz artists from Cuba and around the world: performances, workshops, lectures and open rehearsals.

EATING OUT

It is a sad paradox that a land as fertile as Cuba should have such problems feeding its people. During the so-called Special Period of the early 1990s, food shortages became serious. Rations are still insufficient, with chicken, meat and many other food items hard to come by. However, those with plenty of money (tourists and a small number of Cubans) are immune from hardships and get the most and best of what little is available.

Nevertheless, do not come to Cuba expecting memorable gastronomic experiences. Cuba once had a respectable *criollo* (Creole) cuisine, a fusion of Spanish and African culinary traditions. But many Cubans now have been reduced to eating simple box lunches and sandwiches; the tradition of sitting

Tables outside El Patio restaurant, Havana

down to a mid-day meal common in other Spanish-speaking countries seems all but lost here. Many restaurants have no choice but to offer standard 'chicken or pork' main courses, along with rice and beans. Most hotels play it safe by offering international fare.

Where to Eat

If you're based in a resort, you might face the potentially monotonous reality of eating almost all your meals at the hotel. Large hotels often have not only a main buffet restaurant but also a poolside *parrillada* (grill) and a beachside café.

State-run restaurants are of two types. Those for tourists offer food that is usually edible; you must pay in *pesos convertibles*. Those for Cubans have extremely limited menus and, generally, poor quality; waits are long, and *pesos cubanos* are the accepted currency. In some isolated cities (like Bayamo) it is possible to eat in *peso cubano* establishments very cheaply, as long as you understand that perhaps only one item on the menu will be available and that Cuban diners might look at you as if to say, 'How did you get in here?' Often, however, they will charge in *pesos convertibles* because you are a foreigner.

A third category is the *paladar*, a privately operated restaurant in a private home. These cater to anyone who pays in *pesos convertibles*. For a while they operated clandestinely outside the law, but in 1995 the government legalised them, only to subsequently tax or fine many of them out of existence. The maximum legal number of place settings is limited to 12. The food is often better than in state-owned restaurants, portions are larger, and the cost is generally more reasonable. Frequently you'll be offered a three-course meal, sometimes with a beer or juice included, for a set price. *Paladares* are like small, simple restaurants, usually with menus, that just happen to be on the terrace or in someone's home.

Fruit at a street market

If you are staying at a *casa particular (see page 105)*, you can take advantage of the freshest and best *criollo* food. Families will cook whatever you want, or offer a few staple dishes. Usually you decide in the morning whether you want to eat in and they will shop and cook it for your evening meal. Fortified by a hearty breakfast of fresh fruit, eggs, coffee, juice and bread, these two meals will probably be enough, with just a snack at midday.

In all resort hotels and around Havana, cafés serve sandwiches (almost always ham and/or cheese), but otherwise snacks in Cuba are limited to bad street pizza and box lunches. Picnic food is an even more difficult proposition: hotel shops sell packs of biscuits and chips, while private farmers' markets sell fruit for pesos.

What to Eat

At large hotels, particularly in the resorts, breakfast can be the best meal of the day: a buffet of fresh fruit, fruit juices, cheeses, meats and pancakes. Often there are also egg dishes made to order. In more modest hotels, sandwiches and omelettes are generally the staple fare.

Hotel buffets are also offered at lunch and dinner, and guests with large appetites will find these very good value. The food is 'international' rather than typically Cuban. The surfeit of choices (several salads, piles of bananas, chunks of watermelon, cakes galore, a choice of fish, meat and pasta) might make some travellers uncomfortable, given the ration books most Cubans must adhere to.

Most restaurants serve a Creole Cuban cuisine. Its main staple is rice and beans; you'll find either rice with kidney beans (*moros y cristianos*; 'Moors and Christians') or rice with black beans *(congrís)*, the latter typically served in the east of Cuba. Meat is often *pollo asado* (roast chicken) or *cerdo asado* (roast pork). White fish is commonly presented under the generic label *pescado* and is typically fresh and simply grilled; numerous restaurants also serve lobster at a hefty price (CUC$25–30). Popular side dishes include root vegetables such as *malanga* and *yuca* (cassava) as well as *maduros* or *tostones* (fried plantains). Common desserts are *pasta de guayaba con queso* (cheese with guava paste) and delicious, rich Coppelia ice cream, made all over the country.

Thirst-quencher: the mojito

What to Drink

The national drink is *ron* (rum), produced from cane juice and molasses, the by-products of sugar manufacture. Un-aged rum, called *aguardiente* ('firewater'), has a very high alcoholic content. Five- or seven-year-old rum, darkened and flavoured in oak barrels, is drunk straight or on the rocks.

Cuban cocktails make use of one- or three-year-old white rum. A number have

Cuban beer: a popular brand

achieved folkloric status: Hemingway drank his mojitos (sugar, lime juice, ice, fresh mint, rum and soda water) in La Bodeguita del Medio and his daiquiris (sugar, lime juice and rum blended into crushed ice) in El Floridita. Less exotic is the *Cuba libre*: simply rum and coke, often served with a slice of lime.

National brands of beer include Bucanero, Cristal, Mayabe and Tínima, all very drinkable. Only the more expensive restaurants serve wine. Cuban wine is now produced with the help of Spanish technology, but is in its infancy and best avoided.

For soft drinks, try the wonderfully sweet *guarapo* (pure sugar-cane juice pressed right before your eyes) or *granizado* (a flavoured water-ice in a paper cone from ubiquitous street-side carts). In some towns, you may come across homemade cola stands, where they'll mix three shots of syrup with soda water (a good one is Trinidad's El Gallo Soda). It's amazingly refreshing and only about 5 centavos.

Coffee is one of Cuba's main exports, but you don't always get export-quality coffee. A *café* is served espresso style and traditionally drunk with unimaginable quantities of sugar; *café americano* is weaker and served in a large cup. *Café con leche* is half espresso/half milk. Coffee with a little cream in Cuba is often disappointingly grey.

To Help You Order...

Do you have a table?	**¿Tiene una mesa?**
May I see the menu, please?	**¿Puedo ver la carta, por favor?**
What do you recommend?	**¿Qué me aconseja?**
I'd like …	**Quisiera …**
I'm a vegetarian.	**Soy vegetariano.**

beer	**cerveza**	meat	**carne**
bread	**pan**	salad	**ensalada**
butter	**mantequilla**	sandwich	**bocadito**
cocktail	**cóctel**	shellfish	**mariscos**
coffee	**café**	soft drink	**refresco**
dessert	**postre**	tea	**té**
fish	**pescado**	vegetable	**vegetales/ legumbres**
fruit	**fruta**		
ice	**hielo**	water	**agua mineral**
ice cream	**helado**	wine	**vino**

... and Read the Menu

arroz blanco	white rice	**langosta**	lobster
asado	roast/grilled	**naranja**	orange
bistec	steak	**pan tostado**	toast
camarones	shrimps/ prawns	**papas**	potatoes
cerdo/puerco	pork	**papas fritas**	chips (fries)
congrí	rice and beans	**picadillo**	minced meat
frijoles	beans	**plátano**	plantain
frito	fried	**pollo**	chicken
huevos	eggs	**queso**	cheese
jamón	ham	**tortilla/ revoltillo**	omelette
jugo de fruta	fruit juice		

HANDY TRAVEL TIPS

An A–Z Summary of Practical Information

A

ACCOMMODATION (hotel; alojamiento; casa particular)

Standards and facilities have improved dramatically over the past few years. Cuba's new or restored hotels in resorts and in Havana typically have pools, restaurants, buffets, boutiques, air conditioning and satellite TV. Top resort hotels offer round-the-clock entertainment, while simpler resort hotels offer some in-house entertainment and invariably have a pool. Elsewhere, hotels are much less enticing. Foreigners are billeted in large, Soviet-style concrete eyesores located on the outskirts of towns. Hot water is usually intermittent. Many smaller and inexpensive (peso) hotels do not admit foreigners.

Casas particulares – private accommodation in Cuban homes – are inexpensive alternatives that allow foreigners a view of local life. Prices range from CUC$25–50 per double room in Havana and Santiago to CUC$15–25 in less-visited places; you may be able to bargain down the quoted price for long stays. Be cautious when looking for a *casa*. Avoid intermediaries if possible, and visit the room before committing yourself. Try to stay only at licensed *casas*. Owners of unlicensed *casas* risk ruinous fines if caught, so at least be very discreet if you do use one.

Outside such high periods as Christmas, New Year and Easter, you don't always need advance reservations. It can be difficult getting through to phone numbers in Cuba; for reservations from abroad it is worth checking www.casaparticularcuba.org.

I'd like a room …	**Quisiera una habitación …**
with twin beds/double bed	**con dos camas/cama matrimonial**
What's the price?	**¿Cuál es el precio?**
Is breakfast included?	**¿El desayuno está incluído?**
Is there a private homestay near here?	**¿Conoce una casa particular por aquí?**

AIRPORTS (aeropuerto; see GETTING THERE)

Cuba's main airport is Havana's José Martí International Airport (tel: 07-833 5777 domestic; 07-833 5666 international), located 20km (12 miles) south of downtown Havana. Hotel reservations can be made at the airport's Infotur office *(see page 127)*. Varadero's Juan Gualberto Gómez Airport is 22km (14 miles) west of Varadero. Santiago de Cuba's Antonio Maceo Airport is located 6km (4 miles) south of that city. The airports in Camagüey, Cayo Coco and Holguín are also international, handling charter flights.

On arrival, if you're on a package holiday a bus will transfer you to your hotel. Independent travellers can book transfers through agencies in their own country; otherwise take a taxi. From the airport, avoid expensive Turistaxis (white); yellow Panataxis are much cheaper (CUC$15–20 to downtown Havana; CUC$6–8 to the centre of Santiago). It's a 40-minute trip from José Martí airport to central Havana.

You must pay a departure tax at all airports: CUC$25.

B

BICYCLE HIRE (alquiler de bicicleta)

With the scarcity of public transport, millions of Cubans ride bikes. Most resorts have bikes and mopeds to hire. Many rental bikes are old and have few gears, and serious cyclists intending to tour the country should bring their bikes, as well as plenty of parts and spare tubes.

BUDGETING FOR YOUR TRIP

Compared with the rest of Latin America and other developing countries, Cuba can be surprisingly expensive.

Transport to Cuba. The airfare is likely to be your greatest expenditure, especially if coming from Europe or Asia. It's cheapest to travel outside of high season (mid-Dec to mid-Apr) or on a package tour. Many find combination airfare-hotel deals cheaper than airfare alone.

Accommodation. Hotels in Havana, Santiago and major resorts are expensive, comparable to North America and Europe. In resorts, all-inclusive deals (meals, drinks and entertainment) can be a good option. Private houses *(casas particulares)* are generally inexpensive.

Meals and drinks. State-owned restaurants range from moderate to expensive. Lobster and other shellfish are the most expensive items. *Paladares* (private restaurants in Cuban homes) or home-cooked meals in *casas particulares* are inexpensive alternatives. Alcohol and beer are considerably cheaper than in the UK, and slightly cheaper than in the rest of Europe.

Local transport. Urban public transport is cheap and improving but still crowded and inefficient. Taxis and *bicitaxis* are the best way to get about within cities and resorts; they are inexpensive. Long-distance buses, trains and many domestic flights are also relatively inexpensive.

Incidentals. Entertainment in cabarets and discos is expensive for Cuba (CUC$10–90), and drinks in such nightspots are also much more expensive than in bars and cafés. Gifts like prestigious hand-rolled cigars are expensive, even if much cheaper than they are abroad.

C

CAMPING

There are official campsites in isolated locations all over the island, but they offer basic huts rather than tents. In each major town ask for the Campismo office for local campsites, most of which are used by Cubans on holiday. There are also 21 campsites, hotels or parking sites for tourists using camper vans, with water, power and waste disposal, dotted around the island. Book through an agency abroad, which will issue a voucher for you to present to Campertour (Calle 3 y Malecón, Vedado).

CAR HIRE *(alquiler de automóviles/carros; see also* DRIVING)

There are good reasons for not hiring a car in Cuba. It can be expensive, petrol (gasoline) is pricey by North American standards (although not when compared to the UK), and rental firms are often inefficient and difficult to deal with in the event of car damage or other problems. If you wish to hire a car in one place and return it in another, you must pay the cost of having it returned to its origin. Long-distance buses are reliable and, along with tour buses, go to most places of interest, but only a hire car will allow you to go anywhere you wish, when you wish. To hire a car, you must be at least 21 and have had a year's driving experience. You will need a national or international licence.

Cuba has none of the major international rental agencies. However, there are good local hire firms with offices throughout the island. Here are the main ones, with Havana (07) contact numbers. Least expensive are Vía Rentacar (tel: 204 3606; www.gaviota-grupo.com), MiCar (tel: 204 2444) and Havanautos (tel: 203 9658; www.havanautos.com). More expensive are Panautos (tel: 55 3298), Cubacar (tel: 835 3727; www.cubacar.info) and Rex (tel: 273 9166; www.rex-rentacar.com). See also www.carrentalcuba.com.

Rates range from CUC$40 to $130 per day for unlimited mileage. Insurance must be paid locally even if you have prepaid the car hire abroad. If there is any damage to the car, you must pay the first few hundred dollars-worth of repair unless you prove the accident wasn't your fault. You must leave a cash or open credit-card guarantee to cover for this eventuality. Inspect the car before you set off to identify existing dents and scratches.

I'd like to rent a car …	**Quisiera alquilar un auto/carro …**
for a day/a week	**por un día/una semana**
Fill it up.	**Llénelo, por favor.**

CLIMATE

Cuba has a subtropical climate: hot and humid. The chart below shows the average daily temperature in Havana. For beach lovers and sight-seers, November to May is the ideal time to visit, though there is plenty of sunshine year-round. Hurricane season lasts from June until the end of November. The more active should avoid the height of summer, when it's debilitatingly hot and wet. The mountains are cooler and the south and east drier and warmer. Oriente, the area around Santiago, can be wickedly hot – much hotter than the western region.

	J	F	M	A	M	J	J	A	S	O	N	D
°C	22	22	23	25	26	27	28	28	27	26	24	22
°F	72	72	73	77	79	81	82	82	81	79	75	72

CLOTHING

During the day you'll rarely need more than shorts and a T-shirt (and swimsuit). In towns, wear walking shorts or long trousers. At night in winter, a light sweater or jacket may be needed. In upmarket hotels, restaurants and nightclubs, men are expected to wear a collared shirt and trousers and women are required to dress equally smartly.

COMPLAINTS

Package holidaymakers with a complaint should seek their company's local representative. If the complaint is serious, make a written and (if appropriate) photographic record, and send this to your tour operator when you go home. In addition to asking to see the manager (*jefe/gerente/director*), another course of action which often gets results is to ask for the complaints and suggestions (*quejas y sugerencias*) book.

CRIME AND SAFETY (see also EMERGENCIES and POLICE)

Cuba is a remarkably safe place in which to travel – one of the safest anywhere. The crime that does exist is generally directed at possessions rather than people, so place temptation out of sight. Most top hotels provide safes, though usually with a rental charge.

City streets at night feel more dangerous than they actually are because they are so poorly lit. The one area where you should be wary of purse-snatchers is in Old Havana, particularly on Calle Obispo and the grid of streets south of it to the train station. Central Havana west of the Prado to the Hotel Deauville also has a bad reputation.

I want to report a theft.	**Quiero denunciar un robo.**
my wallet/handbag/passport	**mi cartera/bolso/pasaporte**
my camera	**mi cámara**
safe (deposit box)	**caja fuerte**

CUSTOMS AND ENTRY REQUIREMENTS (aduana)

All visitors need a passport *(pasaporte)* that expires more than six months after your scheduled departure from Cuba and a return ticket.

Tourists also need a tourist card *(tarjeta de turista)* to visit Cuba. If you're travelling on a package holiday, the tour operator will arrange your tourist card for you. If travelling independently, contact your country's Cuban embassy; tourist cards (US$20–35 depending on the country) are also available from airline and travel agencies. The card is valid for 30 days. If you want to stay longer once in the country, you have to go, in person, to the Havana Immigration Office, Factor y Final, Nuevo Vedado, open 8.30am–noon. Business travellers require an official business visa from the nearest Cuban consulate, which can take several weeks; a letter of invitation is usually required.

The US trade embargo does not permit American citizens to spend money in Cuba without special permission. There are general and specific licences for government officials, representatives of international organisations, members of educational or cultural

institutions, Cuban-Americans, journalists, religious or aid workers, researchers and athletes. Those covered by a general licence need
no application or permission. Those wishing to travel officially with
a specific licence should seek permission from the Licensing Division, Office of Foreign Assets Control (1500 Pennsylvania Avenue
NW, Washington, D.C. 20220, tel: 202-622 2480) before contact-
ing the Cuban Interests Section in Washington, D.C., for a visa.

*Any US citizen who travels to Cuba without authorisation by
entering through a third country does so illegally.* Fines are established at up to US$250,000. Upon your return you might be
harassed and have Cuban purchases confiscated. You might also be
taken to court, so it is best to cover your tracks. However, Cuba
welcomes American visitors. Cuban immigration officials do not
stamp passports; they stamp only your tourist card instead.

Restrictions for importation of goods into Cuba are: 200 cigar-
ettes or 50 cigars or 250g tobacco; two bottles of spirits. US citizens
travelling on a general or specific licence can import up to US$100
worth of cigars for personal use. There is no restriction on the amount
of dollars you can bring into the country, although officially you may
not depart Cuba with more than US$5,000 in cash.

| I have nothing to declare. | **No tengo nada que declarar.** |

D

DRIVING

Road conditions. There is little traffic outside of town centres.
Most main roads are paved and in fairly good condition, although
they are not well signposted. The Autopista Nacional (motorway)
runs from Havana west to Pinar del Río and east to Sancti Spíritus. A number of rural roads are not paved. Beware of potholes:
some are big enough to cause real damage. Other hazards are

cyclists, hidden railway crossings and wandering livestock. Driving at night is not advisable.

Rules and regulations. To drive, you must be 21 and have a valid driver's licence. Drive on the right. Speed limits, strictly enforced, are 100km/h (62mph) on the highway (motorway), 90km/h (56mph) on other open roads, 60km/h (37mph) on smaller rural roads and 40km/h (25mph) in urban areas. You are likely to get an on-the-spot fine if caught breaking the speed limit. Insurance is mandatory, as is wearing seatbelts. It's common practice to sound your horn when passing to let vehicles without rearview mirrors know what's happening.

Fuel *(gasolina)*. Cupet stations are spread throughout the country and are open 24 hours. They are not self-service. Petrol or diesel must be paid for in CUC$. The quality of regular petrol is poor, and many rental companies insist that you purchase expensive *'especial'* fuel.

stop	**pare**	give way (yield)	**ceda el paso**
caution	**cuidado**	one-way	**dirección única**
no parking	**no parqueo**	danger	**peligro**

car registration papers	**permiso de circulación**
driver's licence	**licencia de manejar**
How do I get to … ?	**¿Cómo se puede ir a … ?**
Is this the right street for … ?	**¿Es ésta la calle que va a … ?**
Is this the highway (road) to … ?	**¿Es ésta la carretera hacia … ?**
May I park here?	**¿Se puede aparcar aquí?**
Full tank, please.	**Llénelo, por favor.**
I have a flat tire.	**Tengo la goma ponchada.**
My car has broken down.	**Mi carro tiene problemas mecánicos.**

E

ELECTRICITY

Electrical appliances in hotels operate on either 110 volts or 220 volts. Most outlets accept flat-pin plugs, some round-pin plugs. Take an adapter; a converter might also be necessary.

What's the voltage?	¿Cuál es el voltaje?
adaptor/a battery	un adaptador/una pila

EMBASSIES

Canada: Calle 30, no. 518, e/ 5 y 7, Miramar, Havana, tel: (07) 204 2516, (07) 204 2538.
UK: Calle 34, no. 702/4, e/ 7 y 17, Miramar, Havana, tel: (07) 204 1771. The UK embassy also represents New Zealand interests and will help Australian and Irish citizens in an emergency.
US: The US has an Interest Section (in Swiss embassy): Calzada e/ L y M, Vedado, Havana, tel: (07) 333 551. For travellers, this office acts in the same way as an American embassy.

EMERGENCIES (see also HEALTH AND MEDICAL CARE and POLICE)

Asistur, a state-run organisation, helps foreigners with medical or financial problems and is affiliated with a number of international travel insurance companies. For a 10 percent commission, they can negotiate a cash advance if provided with bank details overseas. They can also help to find lost luggage and issue travel documents. Asistur's main office is at Paseo del Prado, 208 e/ Colón y Trocadero, Old Havana, tel: (07) 866 8527. There's also an office in Santiago at Hotel Casa Granda, tel: 68 6600. All offices open 24 hours.
Useful telephone numbers: In Havana, police 820 116, fire brigade 811 115, ambulance 405 093. In Varadero, Trinidad and Santiago dial 116 for the police.

fire	**fuego**
Help!	**¡Socorro!**
Look out!	**¡Cuidado!**
Thief!	**!Ladrón!**

G

GAY AND LESBIAN TRAVELLERS

Cuba is not as virulently anti-gay as are many parts of Catholic Latin America. In fact, since the 1980s Cuban society has become considerably more tolerant and inclusive. Still, discrimination and harassment exist, though they are unlikely to affect most gay travellers. *Jineteros* (male prostitutes) targeting gays are common. Areas known to be popular include the Malecón, the bars in Old Havana, and the bars and restaurants around the Coppelia ice cream park in Vedado.

GETTING THERE (see also AIRPORTS)

Most flights into Cuba are charters. From Canada, regularly scheduled flights to Cuba leave from Montreal or Toronto, taking around four hours. There are also departures from Vancouver, Halifax and Ottawa. Charters arrive at Havana, Varadero and several other airports convenient to beach resorts. From the UK, scheduled flights fly from London and Manchester to Havana (although only Virgin Atlantic flies direct, others go via Paris or Madrid). There are also charter flights to Varadero, Holguín and Camagüey (Playa Santa Lucía and Guardalavaca). From Australia and New Zealand, the options include travelling through Canada, Mexico or other points in Latin America.

For those travelling legally to Cuba, regular flights to Havana from the US originate in Miami and New York. If you have authorisation to travel to Cuba, contact Marazul Tours (tel: 800-223 5334; www.marazulcharters.com).

Those wishing to circumvent travel restrictions from the US usually go through Canada (Toronto, Montreal, Vancouver), Mexico (Mexico City, Mérida, Cancún), Bahamas (Nassau) or Jamaica (Kingston, Montego Bay). Branches of Havanatur handle tourist cards as well as roundtrip air tickets on Cubana Aviación. Their offices are in the Bahamas (tel: 242-326 8643), in Toronto (tel: 905-882 0136), in Montreal (tel: 514-522 0358) and in Mexico City (tel: 525-559 3907). Similar arrangements can be made through Canadian, Jamaican and Mexican airlines and travel agencies.

GUIDES AND TOURS

Most still come to Cuba on package tours, which may include a group excursion or two. If you wish to travel independently and have found a hotel-airfare package that is cheaper than separate arrangements or airfare alone, you are not obligated to go along with the group once in Cuba. Plenty of people check into their resort hotels and take off on their own. The most popular and straightforward way of exploring Cuba is on group excursions. However, these trips – available in any tourist hotel and led by English-speaking tour guides – may insulate you from the most interesting aspects of Cuban life. You can reach virtually the whole island from any resort on excursions; most are flexible and will allow you to break up a daytrip and stay overnight if you wish to explore on your own. Freelance 'guides', offering to take you to *casas particulares* and *paladares* (privately run lodgings and restaurants) or obtain cigars and prostitutes, are omnipresent in Cuba.

H

HEALTH AND MEDICAL CARE (see also EMERGENCIES)

Cuba's national health system has made it one of the healthiest countries in the developing world. There are no mandatory vaccinations required for travel to Cuba; nonetheless, some health professionals recommend vaccinations against typhoid and hepatitis A.

Although Cuban water is chlorinated, tap water is not generally safe to drink. Bottled mineral water *(agua mineral)* is widely available and recommended. The most likely source of food poisoning is from unhygienic hotel buffet food. Cuban food is very plain, and upset stomachs are less common than in many other countries.

The Cuban sun can burn fair-skinned people within minutes. Use plenty of sunscreen and wear a hat. It's also easy to become dehydrated, so be sure to drink plenty of water. Mosquitoes are a menace from dusk to dawn in coastal resorts. Air conditioning helps keep them at bay, but apply insect repellent.

If you need to see a doctor, contact your hotel's reception desk. Large resort hotels have their own doctor. All the island's main resorts have an international clinic *(clínica internacional)*, as do Havana, Santiago de Cuba, Cienfuegos and Trinidad. Medical treatment in Cuba is excellent and free for Cubans. Foreigners, however, must pay. Such treatment is expensive, so proper insurance is essential; make sure your health insurance has appropriate coverage.

Every town has an all-night pharmacy *(farmacia)*. The range of medicines has become severely limited. Resorts have better-stocked international pharmacies, though prices can be astronomical. Bring all the medicines you might need during your stay, including sunscreen, mosquito repellent, vitamins, contraceptives and insect-bite cream.

I'm sick.	**Estoy enfermo(a).**
Where's the nearest hospital?	**¿Dónde está el hospital más cercano?**
Call a doctor/dentist.	**Llame a un médico/dentista.**

HITCH-HIKING *(coger botella* or *pedir botella)*

Although hitching a ride in Cuba is easy and safe, it is not recommended because of the possibility that police may fine your benefactor on suspicion that he's earning dollars illegally. If you're looking to hitch, the biggest problem you'll encounter is the paucity of vehicles (at least outside the major cities). If you're driving a hire car, giving a Cuban a lift is recommended: it's a great way to meet people and learn about their lives (provided you know some Spanish), and your hitch-hiker's local knowledge will help you stay on the right road.

HOLIDAYS *(días festivos)*

The following days are public holidays in Cuba:

1 January	Anniversary of the Triumph of the Revolution: Liberation Day
1 May	International Workers' Day (Labour Day)
25–27 July	National Rebellion Day (26 July)
10 October	Commemorates the beginning of the War of Independence

L

LANGUAGE

The official language is Spanish, but Cuban Spanish is spoken fast; consonants and whole endings of words might be swallowed. The language is more rhythmic and Caribbean-accented in Oriente.

Increasing numbers of Cubans are learning English, and many people in the tourist industry are fluent, but you will most likely need some Spanish, especially outside tourist hotels and major resorts.

The *Berlitz Latin-American Spanish Phrase Book & Dictionary* includes over 1,200 phrases useful for travellers.

M

MAPS

The best road map of Cuba is 'Guía de Carreteras' by the Directorio Turístico de Cuba (on sale in Cuba for CUC$6). Other maps are Hildebrand's 'Urlaubskarte Cuba' (1:1,100,000) and Freytag and

Berndt's 'Kuba/Cuba' (1:250,000); the latter is less up-to-date but has useful city plans. Individual city-centre maps cost CUC$1–2. Hotels and bookshops in Havana and Santiago sell reasonable maps.

MEDIA

You will not receive much outside news in Cuba, although many tourist hotels offer CNN. You might find a stray European newspaper at major hotels in Havana or resorts, but it's not likely. The main national newspaper, *Granma,* is the mouthpiece of the government. A weekly *Granma* international edition is published in English, French and German, with cultural features of tourist appeal. Other national newspapers include the weekly *Trabajadores* ('Workers') and *Juventud Rebelde* ('Rebel Youth'). *Bohemia*, a respected monthly magazine founded in 1908, has in-depth analysis of contemporary Cuba and the world as seen through Cuban eyes.

Radio Taíno (1160 AM), a tourist-oriented music station with some broadcasts in English, is most easily heard around Havana. Tune in to the American Forces Network around Guantánamo on 102.1 FM and 103.1 FM for insights into life in the US naval base.

Of the five state-run television channels, one, Cubavision International, can only be seen on cable TV and is on air 24 hours a day.

MONEY

Currency. Cuba has two currencies, the *peso cubano* (CUP), or national peso, and the *peso convertible* (CUC), or convertible peso. The latter is the one which tourists use most of the time, as it is fully exchangeable for foreign currencies. Tourists have to use the *peso convertible* for all payments such as restaurant bills, hotel bills (if not paid in advance), transport and souvenirs. The only time *pesos cubanos* are needed is in very out of the way places, for street food, snacks or in a rural market, or if you take a local bus. Local town buses cost 20–40 centavos and you are unlikely to need to exchange more than US$5 into *pesos cubanos* for a two-week stay. Spend all your CUCs before you leave the island, as they can't be exchanged outside Cuba. The only place in Cuba where you can change pesos into other currencies is at Havana airport and there could be hold ups.

Currency exchange. For accounting purposes, the *peso convertible* is fixed at US$1 = CUC$1, but in 2004 a 10 percent tax was introduced on all US dollar exchange transactions, followed in 2005 by a revaluation of the peso which affected all currency exchange. Tourists now get 18 percent less when they exchange US dollars (US$1.08 = CUC$1 plus 10 percent tax) and 8 percent less for the Canadian dollar, euro or sterling. You are no longer allowed to pay for anything in foreign currencies, although you can use euros in Varadero. There are banks and *casas de cambio* (exchange houses, called a CADECA) where you can exchange your money. There is no black market. If you want to buy *pesos cubanos*, the rate is CUC$1 = CUP24.

Credit cards (*tarjetas de crédito*). An increasing number of outlets accept credit cards, including many tourist shops, upmarket hotels and restaurants, airlines, petrol stations and car hire companies. American Express is not accepted anywhere, nor are any other credit cards issued in the United States; most Americans will thus need to fund their entire trip in cash. Even Europeans may find their credit cards have been issued by an American bank such as MBNA although the company name is non-US. For example, a Virgin Mastercard is not accepted in Cuba. Nobody should rely solely on credit cards, as not everybody accepts them and, even if they do, telephone lines are sometimes out of action so payments cannot be processed. For large credit card payments, you will be asked to show your passport. Cuba remains a largely cash *(divisa)* economy.

Traveller's cheques (*cheques de viajero*). Traveller's cheques in dollars are accepted (in places that usually also accept credit cards), but they must not be American Express or others drawn on US banks. The easiest way to change traveller's cheques into pesos is at hotels; at a bank or CADECA, you'll need your passport and the official receipt from the cheque-issuing institution. Commission rates are 2–4 percent. If you've mistakenly arrived in Cuba with American Express traveller's cheques, Asistur *(see page 113)* can cash them for a 10 percent commission.

ATMs. Cuba has a growing network of automatic teller machines in cities. Your hotel will know if ATMs are in place by the time of your trip. Several banks (Banco Financiero is one) and CADECAs give over-the-counter cash advances on credit or debit cards on production of a passport, but charge high commission.

Do you accept traveller's cheques?	**¿Cheques de viajero?**
May I pay with a credit card?	**¿Se puede pagar con tarjeta?**
How much is that?	**¿Cuánto es?**

OPENING HOURS

Offices are usually open weekdays from 8am to 5pm, with a one-hour lunch break. Some are open on Saturday mornings, from 8am to noon or 1pm. Banks are typically open weekdays from 8.30am to 3pm.

Some museums open daily, but most close for one day (usually Monday) and also close on Sunday at noon or 1pm. Typical museum hours are 9am (sometimes 8am or 10am) until 5pm (sometimes 4pm or 6pm). Regardless of when you go, you'll find several closed for renovations; make inquiries before travelling a long way.

Restaurants do not typically stay open late; most close their doors around 10pm or even earlier. More modest restaurants often stop serving earlier, as they run out of food. The great exception is *paladares,* which are usually open from noon to 11pm or midnight.

P

POLICE *(policía)*

Most police are helpful and friendly, even though they occasionally harass Cubans (or, specifically, anyone of dark skin colour who might be assumed to be Cuban) accompanying foreigners. If you are robbed, make sure you get a police report, a time-consuming affair.

> Where's the police station? **¿Dónde está la comisaría de policía?**

POST OFFICES *(oficina de correos)*

You can buy stamps *(sellos)* with *pesos convertibles* at hotels, although this costs more than if you buy them with *pesos cubanos* at post offices. Some stamps are not sticky and you have to ask a post office or hotel desk for glue. Cuba's post system is unreliable and slow. Postcards *(tarjetas postales)* sent to Europe take from two weeks to a month or more to arrive. Mail sent from abroad often fails to reach its destination.

Post offices are generally open weekdays 9am to 5pm and Saturday 9am to 3pm. You'll find post offices in every rural town; cities have several branches. In Havana, the best one to use is the one in the Hotel Havana Libre in Vedado (Calles L and 23). More efficient mailing services are available through DHL Worldwide Express, with offices in several cities. In Havana, there's one in the Hotel Havana Libre.

PUBLIC TRANSPORT

Taxis. There are several classes of taxis, which are your best option for travel within cities and resorts. State taxis are metered and fares are paid in *pesos convertibles*. White Turistaxis, OK Taxis and Habanataxis are ubiquitous wherever tourists congregate; they are the nicest and most expensive. Yellow taxis with blue markings are Panataxis, which are metered and are much cheaper; they can be hailed at major tourist hotels, at the airport, or summoned by phone: (07) 555 555.

Private taxis (which might or might not be licensed) also circulate. The lumbering vintage American cars with taxi signs (*colectivos* or *máquinas*) have fixed routes and are usually reserved for Cubans, although the smarter versions, owned by the Grancar company, are state-owned and geared towards tourists – in Havana call (07) 338 417980.

You can hire any taxi for a single fare or a day, and private taxis are available for overnight excursions (don't expect bargains). Many owners of private cars (*particulares*) also operate as freelance taxi drivers, although it is illegal. Owners face large fines if caught, so it's best to ride in official taxis. If you do use *particulares*, fix a fee first.

Buses (*guaguas*, pronounced 'wah-wahs'). Buses are the backbone of Cuba's public transport system, but they're not a great option for tourists. There are too few of them, they're uncomfortable, they're usually full when they do arrive, and there is a risk of being pick-pocketed. The wait at bus stops in Havana has been somewhat alleviated by the use of new buses which have replaced the old *camellos* ('camels') in the city, although they are still in use in Havana province.

For travel between cities, towns and resorts of major tourist interest, however, there is a company named Víazul (Av. 26 e/ Av. Zoológico y Ulloa, Nuevo Vedado; tel: 07-881 1413, 881 5652; www.viazul.com). It operates air-conditioned tour buses to Playas del Este, Varadero, Viñales/Pinar del Río, Cienfuegos, Trinidad, Santa Clara, Sancti Spíritus, Ciego de Ávila, Camagüey, Holguín, Las Tunas, Bayamo and Santiago de Cuba. Prices range from CUC$5 (Havana to Playas del Este) to CUC$55 (Havana to Santiago). If you're not hiring a car in Cuba but travelling independently, Víazul is the way to go. It's far more efficient, faster and more reliable than trains. Another company, Astro, also runs long-distance buses but they are slower and less comfortable.

In Varadero, new tourist buses run the length of the beach. Tickets are valid all day and you can hop on and hop off at any of the 47 stops. Smaller buses operate in Trinidad, Jardines del Rey, Guardalavaca, Viñales and Baracoa.

Trains *(trenes)*. Cuba was the first country in Latin America to have a railroad system, but things haven't improved much since it began. Trains can be a real adventure in Cuba, but you'd best be prepared. Journeys are extremely slow, schedules unreliable, and breakdowns are frequent. Trains usually run only on alternate days or a couple of times a week to most destinations. That said, the stations and trains are wonderfully atmospheric. The *especial*, between Havana and Santiago de Cuba, has reclining seats and air conditioning, while snacks are available. It runs every other day, with stops at Santa Clara (CUC$21), Camagüey (CUC$40) and Santiago (CUC$62). The *regular* stops in all provincial capitals, and if it isn't working it is replaced by a bus service. The best service is a *coche motor*, which runs on alternate days from Havana to Camagüey and on to Santiago de Cuba. With only 54–6 seats, it has air conditioning, TV and video. In Havana you can make bookings at the Estación Central, Arsenal y Ejido (tel: 07-860 3163). Make reservations well in advance for most trips.

Domestic flights. Flying in Cuba is the quickest and most reliable form of transport for long trips. It's also good value (flights range from about CUC$35 to $120 each way). Flights fill up fast, so book in advance from your home country if possible. Cubana, the national airline, provides most domestic flights, including those from Havana to Baracoa, Camagüey, Cayo Largo, Ciego de Ávila, Cienfuegos, Guantánamo, Holguín, Nueva Gerona (Isla de la Juventud), Santiago and Varadero. Frequency varies enormously, from several daily flights to Santiago to twice weekly to Baracoa. Tickets can be purchased in Cubana offices around the country or from the main office in Havana on Calle 23 (La Rampa), no. 64 esq. Infanta (tel: 07-833 4446).

Bicycle taxis. Havana's *cocotaxis* are yellow three-wheeled buggies powered by motorcycle engines. They are just as plentiful as car taxis and cost 50 centavos per kilometre. *Bicitaxis,* pedicabs, are a fun way to traverse the city on short trips. Most trips end up costing about as much as a Panataxi (CUC$2–4). Note that only some *bicitaxis* are licensed to carry foreigners; unlicensed ones should not be used.

Horse carts *(coches)*. Due to fuel shortages, in virtually every city except Havana and Santiago there are horses pulling carts and plush little carriages up and down the main streets. Ironically, horse carriages acting as taxis have become a tourist attraction in the resorts.

When's the next bus/train to…?	**¿Cuándo sale el próximo autobús/tren para…?**
bus station	**terminal de autobuses**
What's the fare to…?	**¿Cuánto es la tarifa a…?**
A ticket to…	**Un billete para…**
single (one-way)	**ida**
return (roundtrip)	**ida y vuelta**

R

RELIGION

Roman Catholicism in Cuba is strongly rivaled by Afro-Cuban religions such as *santería (see page 31)*. Many aspects of these religious practices can be experienced by visitors. The government blunted the power and influence of the Catholic Church in the early 1960s, but mass is still said in churches throughout the island, and since the Pope's visit to Cuba in 1998 there has been a resurgence of Catholic practice.

T

TELEPHONE *(teléfono)*

Cuba's country code is 53. In addition, each area of the island has its own area code (for Havana it is 7), but codes change fairly often. To make an international call from your hotel room, dial 8 or 88 before the country code; on card phones dial 119. To make a domestic call, add the area code (for example, 7 for Havana). For interprovincial calls you first have to dial the appropriate prefix (0 to and from Havana, 01 for all other provinces), followed by the area code, then the number itself. When phoning Cuba from abroad, drop the 0 or 01. Dial 113 for the free domestic telephone enquiries service.

Top hotels have direct-dial facilities for all calls. Elsewhere you can make domestic calls on a direct line, but you will need to go through the hotel operator for international calls. International calls from Cuba are very expensive (CUC$2.20–4.40 per minute). As they do everywhere in the world, hotels charge a significant surcharge on calls. To make domestic calls, either use payphones that accept Cuban pesos (5 centavos for 3 minutes) or ETECSA phone cabins, where you can also make international calls. The cabins are glass boxes with banks of phones that take phone cards *(tarjetas)*, which are also sold there (in denominations of 5, 7, 10 and 30 *pesos cubanos*). ETECSA phone cards are available in denominations of CUC$10 to 50, which are much cheaper for calls abroad.

The use of mobile (cellular) phones is on the increase, particularly since restrictions on Cubans owning them were lifted in 2008. All mobile numbers begin with 5 and have 8 digits. To call a mobile from Havana dial 0 and then the number, from other provinces dial 01 and then the number. Area codes are not needed.

I'd like make a telephone call …	**Quisiera hacer una llamada …**
to England/Canada/ United States.	**a Inglaterra/Canadá/ los Estados Unidos.**
reverse-charge call	**cobro revertido**
Can you get me this number in … ?	**¿Puede comunicarme con este número en … ?**
phone card	**tarjeta telefónica**

TIME ZONES

Cuba is five hours behind GMT. It operates on Eastern Standard Time in winter and Daylight Saving Time (one hour later) from April to October.

San Francisco 9am	**Cuba noon**	New York noon	London 5pm	Sydney 2am

TIPPING *(propina)*

In restaurants tip CUC$1–2 per person, or 10 percent. In bars, loose *(peso convertible)* change is acceptable. Tour guides expect at least CUC$2 for their services, and roving musical groups should be given a *peso convertible*. In almost any other situation, a peso is a very generous tip, and loose change might be more appropriate.

TOILETS *(baños)*

It's often best to carry a roll of toilet paper with you at all times in Cuba, as many establishments do not provide their own. Those that do demand a few cents for providing it – fine, if you've got change.

TOURIST INFORMATION

There are official Cuban government tourism offices in Canada and Britain but not in the US:

Canada: 2075 rue University, Bureau 460, Montréal, Québec H3A 2L1, tel: 514-875 8004; 1200 Bay Street, Suite 305, Toronto, Ontario M5R 2A5, tel: (416) 362 0700.
UK: 154 Shaftesbury Avenue, London WC2H 8JT, tel: (020) 7240 6655.

In Cuba itself, there is no centralised system providing tourism information, and reliable information is sometimes hard to come by. Instead, you must rely upon hotels and travel agencies, whose primary function is to sell excursion packages. In Cuba all hotels have a tourism desk *(buró de turismo)*.

Infotur is the only tourist information service, although other state tour operators will help. Infotur contracts out tours and excursions, and sells maps, guides, postcards, magazines, souvenirs and phone cards. They can also make hotel reservations. The main office is at Obispo, 521 e/ Bernaza y Villegas in Old Havana, tel: (07) 866 3333. Other branches are at the airport terminals; Av. Las Terrazas e/ 10 y 11, Playas del Este, tel: (07) 971 261; Av. 5 y 112, Playa, tel: (07) 204 7036; and Obispo y San Ignacio, Old Havana, tel: (07) 863 6884.

If you need a particular address or phone number, ask to see the *Directorio Turístico de Cuba* (Cuban Tourist Directory), usually available in hotel rooms.

W

WEBSITES

Although few Cubans have access to the internet, Cuba is surprisingly well served by the web. From sites about the US embargo and travel restrictions to traveller recommendations, there is a wealth of information.

A few sites worth exploring include the following:

www.dtcuba.com Cuban Tourist Directory site
www.cubaweb.cu Official government site
www.cuba.com
www.cubalinda.com
www.travelnet.cu
www.cuba-junky.com
www.casaparticularcuba.org
www.lahabana.com

Recommended Hotels

The very best hotels are joint ventures with private firms from Spain, Canada and other countries. These are of an international standard. Many others, though, are a notch or two down from what you'd expect in Europe, North America or Asia. At the inexpensive level, hotels are usually quite lacking in ambience and amenities.

Casas particulares – accommodation in private homes – are not only a better-quality and much cheaper alternative to the inexpensive hotels; they allow you a glimpse into unguarded Cuban life. They generally cost CUC$15–35 per room. Your hosts usually also offer breakfast and home-cooked meals at a small extra cost. You'll find a very abbreviated list of recommended private-home *casas* following the regular hotel listings below; however, others are very easy to find.

The price categories below, in US dollars, are for a standard double room, excluding meals, in high season (mid-December to mid-April, July to August). Prices drop by 15–30 percent during other months. All accommodation is paid for in *pesos convertibles*. Only top hotels accept credit cards; remember that credit cards issued by American Express or drawn on US banks are not accepted in Cuba. For reservations it's best to call directly and get a confirmation number or name of the person you spoke with.

$$$$	over $150
$$$	$100–150
$$	$50–100
$	under $50

HAVANA

OLD HAVANA

Ambos Mundos $$–$$$ *Obispo esq. Mercaderes, Habana Vieja, tel: (7) 860 9530, www.habaguanexhotels.com.* Hemingway wrote much of *For Whom the Bell Tolls* in room 511 of this historic hotel (opened in 1920). It's in the heart of Old Havana, on one of its most picturesque streets. The hotel was gloriously restored in 1997, and rooms are nicely decorated. On the ground floor is an airy, lovely piano bar and the rooftop bar offers great views. 50 rooms.

La Casa del Científico $ *Prado 212 esq. Trocadero, tel: (7) 862 4511, fax: (7) 860 0167.* A great budget hotel in a lovingly pre-served late-colonial building that still has all its original features including a magnificent marble staircase. The rooms are simple and bathrooms are private or shared. The opulent dining room and lounge reveal faded glory with a lovely view over the Prado from the balcony. Reservations essential.

Hotel Florida $$–$$$ *Calle Obispo esq. Cuba, Habana Vieja, tel: (7) 862 4127, www.habaguanexhotels.com.* A marvellous colonial mansion built in 1836, achieves affordable luxury. It orig-inally became a hotel in 1885 but reopened only in 1999. It is extremely elegant, with plush public rooms, a lovely courtyard, and a great location just a couple of blocks from the Plaza de Armas. Some rooms have balconies. Piano bar, lobby bar and restaurant. 25 rooms.

Hotel Mercure Sevilla $$$ *Trocadero, 55 e/ Zulueta y Animas, Habana Vieja, tel: (7) 860 8560, fax: (7) 860 8582.* This restored turn-of-the-20th-century establishment, of Spanish and Moroccan inspiration, is again one of the best in the old city. It has a sumptu-ous lobby, magnificent rooftop restaurant and other excellent din-ing options. Guests have included Al Capone, Josephine Baker and Enrico Caruso, and scenes from Greene's *Our Man in Havana* were set here. Rooms are comfortable and stylish. Good pool, gym-nasium. 179 rooms.

Hotel Santa Isabel $$$ *Calle Baratillo, 9 e/ Obispo y Narciso López, Habana Vieja, tel: (7) 860 8201, www.hotelsantaisabel.com.* This small, quiet, gorgeously restored hotel is an 18th-century palace right on the Plaza de Armas, the city's oldest. Sumptuous rooms have period furniture, and the hotel features a lovely courtyard and great views from the roof. Prices include breakfast, served over-looking the Plaza. 27 rooms and suites.

Hostal Valencia $$ *Oficios, 53 esq. Obrapía, Habana Vieja, tel: (7) 867 1037, www.habaguanexhotels.com.* In an 18th-century mansion between Plaza de Armas and Plaza Vieja, this small Spanish-style yellow colonial is utterly charming. One of the city's best deals, it features rooms (no air conditioning) surrounding a delightful green courtyard. Fine Spanish restaurant. Book well in advance. 12 rooms.

NEW HAVANA

Hotel Nacional de Cuba $$$ *Calle O esq. 21, Vedado, tel: (7) 873 3564, fax: (7) 873 5171, www.hotelnacionaldecuba.com.* A classic feature of New Havana, this landmark 1930 hotel rises above the Malecón. Former guests include Hemingway, Churchill, Frank Sinatra, Ava Gardner, Errol Flynn, Marlon Brando and gangsters Meyer Lansky and Lucky Luciano. Rooms are large, and most have sea views. It has a stunning dining room, two pools, a nightly cabaret show, gardens, terraces and bars. Prices include breakfast. 467 rooms.

Tryp Habana Libre $$$ *Calle L esq. 23 y 25, tel: (7) 834 6100, www.solmeliacuba.com.* An iconic tower hotel which opened in 1958 as the Hilton but was renamed in 1959 when it became the Revolutionary headquarters for a few months. Fascinating photos of that time line the hotel lobby. It is now a luxury hotel with lots of facilities including a shopping mall, airline offices, coffee shop, good restaurants and the Cabaret Turquino on the 25th floor with a roof which opens so you can dance under the stars. 572 rooms.

PINAR DEL RÍO PROVINCE

Horizontes La Ermita $–$$ *Carretera de la Ermita, km 2, Viñales, tel: (8) 893 204, fax: (8) 336 091.* This contemporary, low-slung hotel of Spanish colonial design is lacking in service and style, but it has some of the finest views in the country, particularly from the swimming pool. The verdant valley and spectacular sunsets fill the horizon. An enjoyable 20-minute walk from Viñales town. 62 rooms.

Los Jazmines $$ *Carretera de Viñales, km 23.5 (3km from Viñales), tel: (8) 936 205, fax: (8) 936 215.* This pretty hotel on the edge of the beautiful Viñales valley has stupendous panoramic views. Bedrooms with balconies (in need of repair and redecoration), excellent pool. Horse-riding is available, and there are well-organised tours. 62 rooms and 16 small cabañas.

ISLA DE LA JUVENTUD

El Colony $$ *Carretera de Sigueanea, km 16, tel: (46) 398 282, fax: (46) 398 420.* On the coast, 42km (26 miles) southwest of Nueva Gerona, this is an isolated 1950s tourist enclave of exclusive interest to divers. The hotel is adequate but the diving is superb. Lots of activities. 77 rooms.

CAYO LARGO

Sol Pelícano $$$$ *tel: (45) 248 333, www.solmeliacuba.com.* All the hotels on Cayo Largo del Sur are all-inclusive, booked as packages from abroad. This 4-star hotel has all the facilities you could possibly need for a successful beach holiday, offering activities such as diving and lots of entertainment for children. 307 modern, functional rooms and junior suites.

MATANZAS PROVINCE

VARADERO

Meliá Las Américas $$$–$$$$ *Carretera Las Morlas, Playa Las Américas, tel: (45) 667 600, fax: (45) 667 625, www.solmeliacuba. com.* This swanky 5-star hotel is a highly-ranked all-inclusive golf and beach resort offering international quality and facilities. 300 rooms and 120 suites.

Meliá Varadero $$$$ *Autopista del Sur, Playa Las Américas, tel: (45) 667 013, fax: (45) 667 012, www.solmeliacuba.com.* Located next to the Plaza Las Americas Convention Center and Shopping Center, this is an all-inclusive mega-complex with tons of amenities: fountain, pool, five restaurants, disco, shops and more. Direct beach access. 490 rooms.

Mercure Coralia Cuatro Palmas $$–$$$ *Avenida 1ra el 60 y 61, tel: (45) 667 040, fax: (45) 667 208, www.accorhotels.com.* An attractive beachside complex on either side of the road of colonial-style villas and bungalows. Some of the rooms (which can be a little worn) are arranged around an excellent pool. 343 rooms. Convenient for down town, nightlife and restaurants.

Varadero Internacional $$–$$$ *Av. Las Américas, tel: (45) 667 038, fax: (45) 667 246, www.gran-caribe.com.* Varadero's renowned 1950s former Hilton hotel has lost some period features and is now an all-inclusive with dull food, but benefits from the best section of beach on the peninsula. Rooms are large, overlooking the beach, but many are in need of refurbishment. 162 rooms.

ZAPATA PENINSULA

Villa Guamá $ *Laguna del Tesoro, Ciénaga de Zapata, tel: (45) 92979.* Reached by boat, this is one of the most distinctive places to stay in Cuba with replica Taíno village. Thatched huts are spread over interconnected islands in the middle of a swamp. Mosquito repellent essential. Good for birdwatching. Crocodile on the menu.

CENTRAL CUBA

CIENFUEGOS

La Unión $$–$$$ *Ave 31 esq. 54, tel/fax: (43) 551 020.* The building dates from 1869 and has been restored into a hotel, making this the nicest place to stay in the area, but its town centre location means it can be noisy. Facilities include a business centre, gym, courtyard, pool (which can get very crowded), car rental, restaurant and bars.

TRINIDAD

Iberostar Grand Hotel Trinidad $$–$$$ *José Martí y Lino Pérez, tel: (41) 996 070, www.iberostar.com.* Centrally located, this is the best hotel in the area. Good service, good food, lovely renovated old building with balconies overlooking plaza, but no pool or terrace.

CAYO COCO

Tryp Cayo Coco $$$ *Cayo Coco, tel: (33) 301 300, fax: (33) 301 386, www.solmeliacuba.com.* One of Cuba's most attractive resort hotels, a replica of a colonial village amid palm gardens and by a dazzling white beach. Pastel-coloured villas interwoven by a magnificent sculpted pool. Watersports, restaurants, shops. 508 rooms.

CAYO GUILLERMO

Iberostar Daiquirí $$$ *Cayo Guillermo, tel: (33) 301 650, fax: (33) 301 641.* A good, popular, all-inclusive family hotel, with bright, recently refurbished rooms, each with its own balcony. Long, narrow beach, shallow sea. Good food, buffet or themed restaurants, nice pool, excellent service. 312 rooms.

CAMAGÜEY

Gran Hotel $–$$ *Calle Maceo, 67, tel: (32) 292 094, fax: (32) 293 933.* This colonial building in the heart of town has been a hotel since 1937. Handsome lobby and nice suites, refurbished 2008. Most rooms have balconies, but those overlooking the street can be noisy.

PLAYA SANTA LUCÍA

Club Amigo Caracol $$–$$$ *Playa Santa Lucía, tel: (32) 365 158, fax: (32) 365 307.* The resort's prettiest hotel has flower gardens and two-storey villas with fancy bedrooms, each with balcony, sea view and sitting area. Lots of activities and facilities. 150 rooms.

ORIENTE: THE EAST

GUARDALAVACA

Brisas Guardalavaca $$$$ *Playa Guardalavaca, tel: (24) 30218, fax: (24) 30162, www.brisasguardalavaca.com.* This all-inclusive resort offers a choice of restaurants, an attractive pool, direct beach access, and a range of activities. 437 rooms, suites and villas.

SANTIAGO DE CUBA

Hotel Casa Granda $$$ *Heredia, 201 (on Parque Céspedes), tel: (22) 686 600, fax: (22) 686 035.* A grand white building in the heart of Santiago, overlooking the main plaza, this classic hotel is a great place for people-watching, but the rooms are tired and dingy. In its heyday Joe Louis and Graham Greene's 'Man in Havana' stayed here. Terrace bar with great views.

Gran Hotel $ *Enramada 312 e/ San Félix y San Pedro, tel: (0122) 653 020.* Central and convenient for shops and sites of interest, this simple hotel is used as a training school for the hospitality industry, so expect variations in service. Restaurant, snack bar and bar, and only 15 rooms, some of which are triples.

Meliá Santiago de Cuba $$$–$$$$ *Av. de las Américas y Calle M, tel: (22) 687 070, fax: (22) 687 170, www.solmeliacuba.com.* Santiago's most ostentatious hotel, 3km (2 miles) from the centre. Six bars, luxury pool, indulgent buffets and snazzy nightclub. 302 rooms.

PARQUE BACONAO

Club Amigo Carisol Los Corales $$$ *Carretera Baconao, km 31, Playa Cazonal, tel: (22) 356 121, www.cubanacan.cu.* A 3-star hotel at the eastern end of the nature reserve, an hour from Santiago. Bungalows and mini-villas in spacious gardens. Pool, beach, snorkelling, swimming and fishing. Mountain or sea views. 310 rooms.

BARACOA

Hotel El Castillo $$ *Calixto García, Loma del Paraíso, tel: (21) 45165, fax: (21) 45223, www.hotelelcastillocuba.com.* One of Cuba's most charming hotels, converted from one of Baracoa's old forts. Perched on a cliff, it has a fine pool, gardens, mountain views, helpful staff and spacious bedrooms. A real bargain. 34 rooms.

Hostal La Habanera $–$$ *Maceo esq. Frank País, tel: (21) 45273, www.hostallahabanera.com.* This pretty pink building in the town centre was converted to a hotel in 2003 and is designed on traditional lines with an internal courtyard and balconies. Small and stylish, it also has the best restaurant food in Baracoa. 10 rooms.

CASAS PARTICULARES (PRIVATE LODGINGS)

HAVANA

Casa Federico $ *Cárcel 156 e/ San Lázaro y Prado, Old Havana, tel: (7) 861 7817, email: llanesrenta@yahoo.es*. Spacious rooms in an apartment just off the Malecón. Good breakfasts and evening meals; the only drawback is the climb up the 64 stairs. Friendly and helpful hosts; some English spoken.

Mercedes González $ *Calle 21 360 Apto 2A, e/ G y H, Vedado, tel: (7) 832 5846, email: mercylupe@hotmail.com*. Situated in a pleasant area near a park, with two rooms and an abundance of tropical plants. Each room has air conditioning, a good bathroom, TV and fridge; one has a balcony. Meals are available; English is spoken.

TRINIDAD

Casa Colonial Muñoz $ *José Martí, 401, e/ Fidel Claro y Santiago Escobar, tel/fax: (41) 993 673, email: trinidadjulio@yahoo.com*. Colonial house built in 1800; large rooms furnished with antiques, new bathrooms, shady patio and roof terrace. Knowledgeable English-speaking hosts with children and dogs. One of the finest *casas* in Cuba.

Casa López-Santander $ *Camilo Cienfuegos 313, e/ Jesús Menéndez y Julio Antonio Mella, tel: (41) 993 541*. Rooms in an attractive home dating from 1916, with a porch and striking neoclassical façade. Two blocks from Plaza Santa Ana; a 10-minute walk to the Plaza Mayor. Parking, and pleasant patio area.

Hostal Isabel Cristina Prada $ *Fernando Echerri 31, esq. Patricio Lumumba, tel: (41) 993 054*. A colonial house in the centre, near Plaza Mayor. One room has its own street entrance. It's in the main party street, though, so not so good if you want an early night.

SANTIAGO DE CUBA

Casa Hugo-Adela $ *San Basilio, 501, tel: (22) 626 359.* Rambling old house with apartment (kitchenette, private bath, separate entrance) on huge top terrace; spectacular views of the city.

Colonial Tania $ *Santa Lucía 101, e/ Padre Pico y Callejón Santiago, www.casaparticularcuba.org.* Central yet quiet colonial house with high ceilings. Two rooms, each with bathroom, one double, one twin, fridge, air conditioning, terrace with harbour views. Meals available.

Casa Marta Franco $ *Corona, 802 bajos e/ San Carlos y Santa Rita, tel: (22) 651 882.* Ideal location in the heart of the old city, only 100m from the cathedral. Ground floor apartment of a friendly host family. The two guest rooms share a bathroom. The food is good, fresh and wholesome, served in the family room.

VIÑALES

Casa Doña Inesita $ *Salvador Cisneros, 40, tel: (8) 793 297.* Simple lodging in an upstairs apartment with two bedrooms sharing sitting room, bathroom and balcony. Doña Inesita prepares meals using ingredients from her garden. She even grows and roasts her own coffee.

SANTA CLARA

Hostal Florida Center $ *Candelaria, 56 e/ Colón y Maceo, tel: (42) 208 161.* Colonial house on one level around a leafy courtyard. The charming host is an excellent cook. The rooms contain antique furniture but have modern luxuries as well.

BARACOA

Casa Colonial Lucy $ *Céspedes, 29 e/ Rubert López y Maceo, tel: (21) 643 548.* Pretty colonial house run by the efficient Lucy, who can arrange excursions and knows what is going on. Lovely rooms and a pleasant roof terrace with terrific views over the town to the sea. Good food available, local specialities served.

Recommended Restaurants

The dining choices in Cuba are hotels, state-owned restaurants, *paladares* (private restaurants in people's homes) and *casas particulares*. State restaurants can be overstaffed, the service slow and the menu unreliable. *Paladares* can be better, serving typical Cuban food, but outside Havana their numbers have fallen. The freshest and best Cuban food can be found in *casas particulares*, where they shop daily and prepare meals with prior arrangement. Arrive at restaurants by 8pm or earlier, as certain offerings might be sold out later.

The price categories below indicate the per-person cost for a three-course meal, excluding drinks, tips and shellfish (the latter is always the costliest dish on the menu). Only restaurants in top hotels take credit cards, and American credit cards are not accepted *(see page 119)*. For foreign visitors, it is very difficult to pay for meals in *pesos cubanos*.

$$$	over CUC$25
$$	CUC$12–25
$	under CUC$12

OLD HAVANA

La Bodeguita del Medio $$$ *Empredado, 207 e/ San Ignacio y Cuba, tel: (7) 867 1374.* Open daily for lunch and dinner until late. Now in its seventh decade, this scruffy, graffiti-scrawled den has played host to celebrities from Sinatra to Salvador Allende. Now a stream of tourists sips mojitos along with Creole cuisine.

Café del Oriente $$$ *Plaza de San Francisco, tel: (7) 860 6686.* Open daily for lunch and dinner (bar-café open 24 hours). This slick international restaurant in a beautiful colonial mansion is where to go for that dress-up, blow-out meal. Extensive wine list.

La Divina Pastora $$–$$$ *Fortaleza de la Cabaña, tel: (7) 860 8341.* Open daily for lunch and dinner. Take the tunnel under the harbour to reach this stylish restaurant, set in a beautifully converted old battery by the waterside below the fort. Great view of Havana skyline. Fish and seafood dishes and correct, swift service.

La Paella $$–$$$ (Hostal Valencia) *Oficios, 53 esq. Obrapía, tel: (7) 867 1037.* Open daily for lunch and dinner (until late). The city's best Spanish food – featuring rice dishes like paella, naturally – is found at this charming inn. Comfortable and friendly; good value.

Paladar La Julia $ *O'Reilly 506A, tel: (7) 627 438.* A traditional *paladar* offering huge portions of Cuban food, including good rice and beans. Popular, so come early or make a reservation.

El Patio $$–$$$ *Plaza de la Catedral, tel: (7) 867 1034.* Open 24 hours. One of the capital's romantic settings for a meal, in one of Havana's most splendidly painted and restored colonial courtyards. Creole fare is decent, but it can't match the surroundings. The popular drinks terrace looks out on the Plaza de la Catedral.

Café Taberna Beny Moré $ *Mercaderes esq. a Teniente Rey (corner of Plaza Vieja), tel: (7) 861 1637.* Open daily for lunch and dinner. In what was Havana's oldest café, Beny has been newly renovated in the exact style of the original. Live bands day and night; livelier at lunch.

CENTRAL HAVANA AND NEW HAVANA

1830 $$$ *Calzada y Av. 20, Vedado, tel: (7) 533 090.* Open noon until midnight. A popular restaurant right at the mouth of the river, a great location for weddings and family celebrations. International food well prepared. Dinner is followed by a cabaret at 10pm and lots of live music.

El Aljibe $$ *Av. 7 e/ 24 y 26, Miramar, tel: (7) 204 4233.* Open daily for lunch and dinner. One of the best dining experiences in the capital is at this thatched-roof restaurant out in Miramar, offering top-flight Creole cooking. The speciality is the all-you-can-eat lemony chicken *(pollo asado El Ajibe)*, with salad, plantains, chips, rice and beans. Popular with international businesspeople and diplomats.

La Guarida $$ *Calle Concordia, 418, e/ Gervasio y Escobar, Centro Habana, tel: (7) 863 7351, www.laguarida.com.* Open daily for lunch and dinner. The most famous *paladar* in Havana, this atmospheric place was where much of the Cuban film *Fresa y Chocolate* was filmed. Creative, wonderfully prepared food.

La Torre $$$ *17 y M, Vedado, tel: (7) 553 088.* At the top of the FOCSA building with great views all over Havana. The restaurant has a high class kitchen serving French and international food. Open for lunch and dinner, you can stay on till late for drinks at the bar.

COJÍMAR

La Terraza $$ *Calle Real y Candelaria, tel: (7) 559 232.* Founded in 1925, this charming waterside fish restaurant was once Hemingway's favourite. Grilled fish and paella; nice bar.

VIÑALES

Casa de Don Tomás $–$$ *Salvador Cisneros, tel: (8) 793 114.* Open for lunch and dinner. In a handsome colonial building dating from 1879. Food average but it is pleasant to sit on the veranda overlooking the garden while listening to live music and enjoying a cocktail.

Ranchón San Vicente $$ *Carretera a Puerto Esperanza Km. 38, Pinar del Río, tel: (8) 893 200.* A rustically built country restaurant, surrounded by a farm dedicated to the breeding of game cocks. Open until 4pm. Try the broiled pork for lunch.

VARADERO

El Aljibe $–$$ *Av. 1ra. Calle 36, tel: (45) 614 019.* Open daily for lunch and dinner. The sister restaurant of one of Havana's best dining options *(see above)*.

Mansión Xanadú $$$ *Av. Las Américas, km 8.5, tel: (45) 668 482, www.varaderogolfclub.com.* Open daily noon–10.30pm. Grand seaside mansion serving international dishes with variable success.

Lunchtime snacks available on the terrace. On the third floor the Casa Blanca Panoramic Bar has cocktails and live music.

CIENFUEGOS

Palacio de Valle $$ *Calle 37 esq. 2, Punta Gorda, tel: (43) 551 226.* Open daily for lunch and dinner. Next to the Hotel Jagua, this ornate 19th-century Moorish palace *(see page 58)* has a ground-floor restaurant serving reasonable seafood and paella. Rooftop bar.

TRINIDAD

El Jigüe $–$$ *Rubén M. Villena esq. P. Guinart, tel: (419) 994 315.* Open daily for lunch and dinner. An attractive colonial house with a gloriously painted façade, and terrace leading on to one of Trinidad's prettiest squares. International and Cuban dishes. Live music.

Sol y Son $ *Calle Simón Bolívar, 283, e/ Frank País y José Martí.* Open daily for lunch and dinner. A colonial house with an entryway that might be an antiques shop and peaceful courtyard, offering such dishes as *cerdo borracho* (drunken pork, with rum) and stuffed fish.

CAMAGÜEY

Campana de Toledo $ *Plaza de San Juan de Dios, tel: (32) 295 888.* Open daily for lunch. Good – if not memorable – Spanish and Creole fare in one of the city's prettiest courtyards. Live music.

GUARDALAVACA

El Ancla $$ *Playa Guardalavaca, Banes, tel: (24) 30237.* Open daily for lunch and dinner. Seafood platters and pastas and a waterside cocktail terrace in a fabulous site at the eastern end of the beach (cross the beach and river to reach it). A lovely spot for a lobster lunch.

Compay Gallo $$ *3km (2 miles) from Holguín on the way to Guardalavaca, Banes, tel: (24) 30132.* Open daily for lunch and dinner. This rural hacienda makes an excellent stop on a day trip from the beach. Chicken is the speciality but the owners also breed pheasants, guinea fowl and quail, so the menu is varied and makes a change from fish and seafood. Live music is usually played.

SANTIAGO DE CUBA

El Morro $$ *Carretera del Morro, tel: (22) 691 576.* Open daily for lunch and dinner. In a superb clifftop location on a vine-covered terrace next to Castillo del Morro, this restaurant might be the best in Santiago, offering excellent Creole fare along with the coastal views.

Santiago 1900 $–$$ *Bartolomé Masó, 354, e/ Hartmann y Pío Rosado, tel: (22) 623 507.* Open daily for lunch and dinner. This spectacular mansion has a beautiful courtyard and two terraces upstairs. You can pay in *pesos cubanos*, which makes a meal absurdly cheap. However, the *criollo* cooking is mostly hit or miss, as are the mojitos.

Sitio de Compay Segundo $$–$$$ *Montenegro, Siboney, tel: (22) 39325.* Along the coast outside Santiago, this is the house where the musician, the late Compay Segundo, of Buena Vista Social Club, was born. Now converted into a restaurant, open for lunch and dinner, serving a range of international and local food.

Tocororo $$$ *Avenida Manduley, 57, esq. 7, Vista Alegre, tel: (22) 641 369.* Open daily for lunch and dinner. As close as Cuba gets to nouvelle cuisine. The setting is a posh villa.

Tropical $$ *Fernández Marcane e/ 10 y 9.* One of the only two legal *paladares* left in Santiago. An open-air dining space on the upper floor. Open for dinner only until late. International style, good food.

BARACOA

La Colonial $ *José Martí, 123, tel: (21) 645 391.* Open daily for lunch and dinner. Of Baracoa's many good *paladares*, this is one of the nicest, with a seductive ambience, a pretty courtyard and such local fare as coconut-flavoured fish-and-rice dishes and sweet *cucurucho* (shredded coconut with fruit flavouring).

INDEX

Berlitz pocket guide

Cuba

Eleventh Edition 2009
Reprinted 2010

Written by Fred Mawer
Updated by Sarah Cameron
Series Editor: Tony Halliday

Photography credits
Anna Mockford and Nick Bonnetti 6, 9, 10,
11, 12, 14, 17, 18, 20, 22, 25, 26, 27, 29, 30, 32,
33, 34, 35, 36–7, 39, 40, 41, 42, 44, 48, 49, 50,
53, 55, 57, 60, 61, 62, 63, 66, 67, 70, 71, 73, 74,
77, 78, 81, 84, 87, 88, 90, 93, 95, 96, 98, 100,
101, 102; Glyn Genin 59, 69; Fred Mawer 65;
Neil Schlecht 47, 82

Cover picture: 4Corners Images

Every effort has been made to provide
accurate information in this publication,
but changes are inevitable. The publisher
cannot be responsible for any resulting
loss, inconvenience or injury.

Contact us

At Berlitz we strive to keep our guides as
accurate and up to date as possible, but if you
find anything that has changed, or if you have
any suggestions on ways to improve this guide,
then we would be delighted to hear from you.

Berlitz Publishing, PO Box 7910,
London SE1 1WE, England.
email: berlitz@apaguide.co.uk
www.berlitzpublishing.com